FOLK SONGS
IN SETTINGS
BY MASTER
COMPOSERS

FOLK SONGS IN SETTINGS BY MASTER COMPOSERS

Herbert Haufrecht

WITH A PREFACE BY VIRGIL THOMSON

FUNK & WAGNALLS   NEW YORK

PREFACE

BY VIRGIL THOMSON

OUR Western music, from the earliest Christian times, has adored to manipulate familiar tunes. Whenever these have been adapted to liturgical use and their words come under Church control, we call them "sacred" and codify them as hymns or chants. In their more primitive state, still secular in their associations, we call them folklore and "collect" them.

Around the year 1200, when music began its still continuing growth as a complex of simultaneous melodies, it became every composer's operating method to wrap his own inventions around some familiar theme song, sacred or secular. Palestrina, like any number of his predecessors, based a Mass on a bawdy song from Crusading times called "L'Homme armé," for the most part concealing the tune with contrapuntal encrustations. But J. S. Bach, in his cantatas and chorale preludes, strove rather to ornament and to throw into maximum relief Lutheran hymn tunes no less secular in origin. All composers, indeed, after Reformation times, tended to treat these ready-made, or "found," materials as jewels.

Now it is not possible to set a jewel otherwise than according to the taste of one's time. And composers have tended to choose folk tunes for their adaptability to being set, not in the style of the music's period—usually unknown—but in that of the composer himself. They have even forced them a little at the joints—as Bach and Haydn and Beethoven all did—to fit them into current metric patterns, or smoothed out with a sharp or flat some modal outline obviously archaic. The value of all such treatments by conscientious and experienced composers lies not in their contributions to ethnography but in the taste of their musical solutions.

Every item in the present collection, from the madrigal-type songs of Sweelinck, Byrd, and Morley to the backwoods patter song of Aaron Copland, is through its musical treatment both a period piece and a personal expression. Certain of them, in fact, have undergone a double transformation, when in Romantic times verses by Robert Burns or Thomas Moore were added to some beloved country tune.

The present volume's distinction derives not only from its being a selection of melodious and poetic gems, but also from the view it offers of musical masters working simply. And how well they do show up, these masters! How clear their harmony! How airy their textures! How imaginative and how suitable their figurations!

How revealing, too, in the comparative scale, are the results of these seemingly routine assignments. Purcell, Beethoven, Haydn, and Mendelssohn are utterly straightforward; Weber, Hummel, and Bruch perhaps less so. All three come out here a trifle slow-flowing, no doubt from overindulgence in chromatics and ostinatos. Coleridge-Taylor's water music, on the other hand, is just right; and Gottschalk's banjo imitations are brilliant. Copland's more primitivistic banjo is no less sagacious for a primitive song, and Britten's evocation of the harp I find wholly delicious. Vaughan Williams' musical references escape me. But Ives's vaudeville-orchestra-like accompaniment for "A Son of a Gambolier" is vastly nostalgic, and comic too. Indeed, only Ives and Copland, among them all, seem to have approached their material with irony.

Most of all, I am grateful to the editor for including so much Beethoven. Among all these settings of "found" music, his Scottish songs are for me the find. And not for any especial Scottishness about them. The Scots of his time would scarce have looked for that. And even today Gaelic ethnomusicology would have little to offer a classical harmonist. It is doubtful, moreover, whether Scottish songs in any harmonizings are likely to catch fire just now, since Scotland itself has ceased to seem romantic. It is for their sheer musical awareness that the Beethoven accompaniments excite me. They are so neat a professional job, and yet so plain, that they summon admiration like a well-baked apple, or like a short letter of the most casual nature from someone who knows really how to write.

ACKNOWLEDGMENTS

I am deeply indebted to Mr. Sidney Beck of the Music Division of the New York Public Library of the Performing Arts at Lincoln Center for his suggestions on the treatment of Renaissance and Baroque music, and to his colleague Mr. Martin Silver for other research. Also, from the Rodgers and Hammerstein Archives of Recorded Sound in the same institution, my thanks to Mr. David Hall for help in compiling the discography. I appreciate the courtesy offered me in the use of the Widener Library of Harvard University and the Boston Public Library with their fine collections of folklore and folk music.

My warm thanks to my very good friend Dr. Norman Cazden for his reading of the manuscript and for his criticism, which stems from his high standard of scholarship. Henrietta Yurchenco, a distinguished critic in the field of folk music, has kindly gone over the material; her views have been valued by me.

Mrs. Ursula Vaughan Williams has graciously granted me permission to reprint her husband's songs. I also wish to acknowledge the cooperation of the following publishers in granting me the use of their copyrighted songs: Boosey and Hawkes, Inc., Peer International Corp., and The H. W. Gray Co., Inc.

But mostly I am grateful to my wife, Betty, for her painstaking consideration of detail and above all for her encouragement and help in making it possible for me to work on this volume.

CONTENTS

II
IRISH SONGS

III
SCOTTISH SONGS

IV
WELSH SONGS

V
AMERICAN SONGS

INTRODUCTION

In recent years there has been a tremendous growth of interest in folk music. Considerable scholarship has been devoted to the field of ethnomusicology, and much has been done by professional and amateur folk singers to revive the old songs and to popularize the new, topical ballads. There is a body of folk music, however, that has been neglected—the folk-song settings by great composers. Their publication has been allowed to lapse; they remain, for the most part, unrecorded; and they are difficult to find even in research libraries. This collection, drawn from diverse sources, is the result of my long-standing interest in the relationship between folk music and the serious composer.

Many of the songs included here were found in various volumes of Scottish, Irish, Welsh, and English songs published in London by George Thomson between 1773 and 1841 and long out-of-print.* The arrangements by Haydn and Beethoven

---

* Thomson's six-volume series appeared as follows:
Volume I, Book 1 (25 songs), 1793; Book 2 (25 songs), 1798; Volume II, Books 3 & 4 (50 songs), 1799; Volume II, Books 5 & 6 (50 songs), 1802; Volume IV, Books 7 & 8 (50 songs), 1805; Volume V, Book 9 (33 songs), 1818; Book 10 (32 songs), 1826; Volume VI, Books 11 & 12 (50 songs), 1841. These volumes are hereafter referred to as the Thompson collection.

selected from it were scored for solo voice (in some songs, for two or three voices) and an instrumental trio of piano, violin, and cello; those by Weber and Hummel, in addition, had a flute. The piano part is quite complete; it is adequate as support for the voice without the other instruments, as printed in the editions of 1822 and 1841.

Another source is Volume II (London, 1792) of William Napier's *Selection of Original Scots Songs,* from which two Haydn songs were culled. These were scored for solo voice with violin and continuo. The figured bass of the harpsichord (often supported by cello, which doubled the bass line) was to be filled in with chords and ornaments during performance, much in the manner of the present-day guitar-playing folk singer who reads a "lead sheet" of melody line with chord names. These simple arrangements were small-scaled, having no introductions, interludes, or concluding passages for instruments.

In the *Fitzwilliam Virginal Book* (an early seventeenth-century manuscript) there are many pieces that are variations on folk tunes; from among these one by Byrd and one by Morley have been selected. These, of course, were keyboard solos to which I have added a vocal line and the text of the song used as the theme for the variations. This same procedure has been followed with the Sweelinck variations on "Von der Fortuna werd' ich getrieben" ("Fortune, My Foe"). Texts from early sources have been added to Purcell's harpsichord "lessons," "A New Irish Tune" and "A New Scotch Tune," and to piano works by Mendelssohn, Gottschalk, and Coleridge-Taylor. All other songs, in their original settings for voice and piano, have been assembled from various publications.

Here, then, is a collection of folk songs in works by composers ranging from late Renaissance and early Baroque to today. The categories are arranged according to national groups and, within that framework, in chronological order. Thus, for example, the section devoted to the songs of England displays in successive order the styles of the virginalists like Byrd, the Baroque of Purcell, the Classic-Romantic lieder of Beethoven, and the contemporary treatments of Vaughan Williams and Britten.

The scope of this book is confined to folk songs in the English language. It must be readily admitted that many of the songs of Ireland, Wales and Scotland were originally sung in the Celtic dialects of Gaelic and Welsh. But in later years, as these groups became bilingual, the melodies were also sung in English. Poets like Thomas Moore and Sir Walter Scott created with the text what many of the composers did with the music—they had taken the rough ore of the peasants' oral tradition and polished it to the sheen of a jewel for the recital hall. Haydn and Beethoven have been criticized for their lack of understanding of the national idiom, and because their arrangements resemble their own style and personality more than the traditional folk style. The latter objection is somewhat justified, but often the two styles achieve a felicitous fusion. This was one of the considerations in my selection.

Haydn made a labor of love out of his assignments for George Thomson. "I boast of this work and by it I flatter myself my name will live in Scotland many years after my death." Thomson confirms this in a letter, saying that Haydn "was so proud of the symphonies [introductions and postludes—*ed.*] and accompaniments which he composed for my melodies as to have the original score of each framed and hung all over the walls of his bedroom."

When Haydn became too old and infirm to continue work on the series, Thomson commissioned Beethoven to carry on. The correspondence between them explains why some of Beethoven's arrangements were not in keeping with the character of the folk song. In a letter of November 23, 1809, Beethoven complains: "Next time please send me the words of the song, since it is absolutely necessary to give them true expression." Six months later, he reiterates this and threatens to drop the assignment unless he receives the words with the tunes. Thomson explains that he can not always comply since the words are "in the heads of the poets." In other words, he was concurrently commissioning poets like Burns and Scott to write adaptations of and additions to the texts.

Fundamentally, Thomson was well-intentioned—he desired to have the intelligentsia and the general public embrace the folk songs of the kingdom. But the many compromises he found necessary often brought him into conflict with poet and composer. His most serious problem, especially with Beethoven, stems from his wish to keep the piano part relatively simple, because, as he explains, "our young ladies . . . don't like and are not able to perform a difficult accompaniment" and the public would feel the complex style inappropriate to the "simple melodies." At another time he writes: "There is not in this country one pianoforte player in a hundred who could make both hands go properly together in the first ritornello; I mean play four notes with one hand and three with the other at the same time" [4 against 3 rhythm—ed.].

Another point of irritation with Beethoven was the fee for the arrangements. In 1812 Beethoven asked for four ducats for each song rather than the agreed upon three, arguing that Haydn had received that sum. Thomson replied that Haydn had never asked for more than two ducats and not a cent for those he revised, whereas Beethoven was paid for revisions; for his last settings, Thomson gave Haydn more on his own volition, "because he had composed much for me truly 'con amore' and because he observed my suggestions with attention and courtesy." In 1813 Beethoven refused to revise nine songs; rather, he begrudgingly made entirely new settings. In another amusing display of irritability in rebuttal to a remark that he asked twice as much money as Leopold Koželuch, Beethoven wrote sarcastically, "I offer my warm congratulations to you and the English and Scottish audiences when they hear it! [Koželuch's arrangement—ed.]. I consider myself, I confess, a cut above Mr. Koželuch (miserabilis!) at this sort of thing, and I do trust you have some discrimination which will enable you to do me justice."

For some reason, Thomson replaced traditional texts with poems of lesser English poets who seem to have had little kinship with the outlook of the Irish, Welsh, and Scottish. In the present collection I have restored the traditional texts and printed them together with those that were set by the composers. In some cases several popular poems are offered for a single song. Thomson occasionally tampered with the tunes or the poets' texts. He even invited Beethoven to make any slight changes in songs "where a passage seems disagreeable to you and which you can improve." Burns often complied with suggested alterations when convinced that they improved his poem. But he refused to permit Thomson to substitute a tune other than that which he had in mind when writing his poem.

Weber composed ten settings for the collection in 1825, but died without completing the remainder for which he had been paid. Thomson then turned to Hummel, who was the last composer to write for him. With these arrangements, which were printed in 1841, Thomson terminated a half-century-long career of music publishing. The fact that he executed the tremendous task of publishing over 315 songs in his spare time and on his spare earnings as a government clerk commands our admiration. His collection is a most significant contribution to folk song literature. We are indebted to him for having been the catalyst for works by many great composers and poets.

Henry Purcell is represented by five songs gathered from an opera, incidental music for the theater, and from harpsichord pieces. Ralph Vaughan Williams and Benjamin Britten are two English composers who have associated themselves with their country's renaissance of interest in its folk music. Both have made many folk song arrangements as well as incorporated the folk idiom in their music. Vaughan Williams has lectured and written a book, *National Music* (London, 1934), in which he expounded his belief that all truly great music is founded upon the folk tradition of the composer's native soil. Samuel Coleridge-Taylor is also an English composer, but his orientation was toward the folk music of the Negro. His affinity with his race was expressed in many works based on songs and spirituals from Africa and America.

Max Bruch wrote *Twelve Scottish Folksongs* that were published by Peters, now out-of-print. I have included three of these tasteful arrangements, which are in his typical Romantic style. His interest in Scottish folk song is also manifest in his *Scottish Fantasy*, Op. 46 for solo violin and orchestra. Probably his enthusiasm for folk music was transmitted to his pupil, Vaughan Williams.

It is only since the 1930s that American composers in greater numbers have delved into our native folk music. Two prominent names among those who were most successful in applying our national music to their works are Aaron Copland and Virgil Thomson.

I have, I believe, compiled a varied group of songs, in terms of both the style of the arrangements and in the content of the music and texts. Here are included love songs, traditional ballads, political songs, broadsides, comic songs, dance tunes, and religious folk songs. Among them are some old favorites as well as little-known songs. Some speak in the vernacular of the common folk, others are in the more polished accents of the poet who collected them. Undoubtedly among the readers will be those who are critical of omissions. Any selection from a vast body of song will ultimately be one of personal choice. I have tried to make this collection representative. By including several songs of individual composers, I hope to give a rounded view of their treatment of folk song.

To the concert-goer and professional or amateur musician this collection may bring a new aspect of the composer, showing a deep regard for folk song. It should be of interest to the ever-growing audience for folk music to learn of the contributions of the great poets and composers to folk song. For the singing recitalist, this volume brings an attractive literature to broaden the repertoire.

It is hoped that this will be the first volume in a series of similar collections devoted to the folk songs of other lands.

—HERBERT HAUFRECHT

FOLK SONGS
IN SETTINGS
BY MASTER
COMPOSERS

I

ENGLISH SONGS

DURING the Elizabethan era, when there was a great flourishing of music and theater, composers were quite familiar with the folk and popular music of their day. Their secular music was in great measure devoted to variations of folk tunes and to dances then current. The Fitzwilliam Virginal Book is one of several collections that contains folk tunes in settings by the masters of that period. Gustave Reese describes the impact of folk music on the instrumental style: "The frequent drawing on folk and dance tunes with their metric nature gives virginal music a rhythmic impetus lacking in purely contrapuntal writing. . . . To be sure, especially in pieces based on songs rather than on dances, polyphonic overlapping is found, but clear-cut phrases are most characteristic." *

A few years after the Restoration, from 1727 and for the next three decades, English composers gave their attention to folk music in the form of ballad operas, in which the airs and choruses were adapted from folk tunes and popular songs. They found in the simplicity of folk song an antidote for the florid artificiality of Italian opera that had dominated the stage.

* Gustave Reese, *Music in the Renaissance,* W. W. Norton and Co., New York, 1954, p. 863.

From 1758 until 1900 there had been a hiatus. But thanks to Cecil Sharp, through his research, promotion, and publications in the early years of this century, there has been a revival of activity among English composers in working with folk music.

According to Sharp's taxonomy, about two thirds of English folk songs are in the major (Ionian) mode; next in quantity is the Mixolydian mode (major scale with lowered seventh). The remainder are either in the Dorian or Aeolian modes (variants of minor). In this collection, "Fortune, My Foe" is an example of the Dorian mode; "The Basket of Eggs" is in the Aeolian; and "Salisbury Plain" combines the two.

1

FORTUNE, MY FOE

Von der Fortuna werd' ich getrieben

JAN PIETERSZOON SWEELINCK (1562–1621)

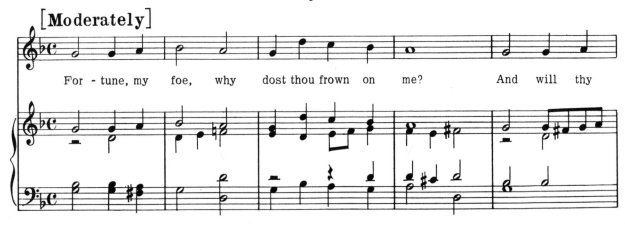

For - tune, my foe, why dost thou frown on me? And will thy

fa - vours nev - er bet - ter be? Wilt thou, I say, for -

ev - er breed my pain, And wilt thou not re - store my joys a -

MUSIC SOURCE: *Jan Pieterszoon Sweelinck. Werken voor orgel en clavecimel*, Max Seifert, ed., Amsterdam, 1894.

Vocal line and text added by the editor. Text from William Chappell, *Old English Popular Music*, London, 1893.

gain?   Wilt thou I say,   for - ev - er breed my pain,

And   wilt thou not re - store my joys a - gain?   2. For - tune hath

wrought me   grief and great an - noy;   For - tune hath false - ly

stole my love a - way,   My   love and joy   whose sight did make me

glad; Such great mis-for - tunes__ nev-er young__ man had;

My love and joy whose sight did make__me__ glad; Such great mis-

for - tunes__ nev-er young man had. How could I bless thee,

could'st thou take a - way My life and in - fa -

my both in one day? But this in

bal - lads will sur - vive I know,

Sung to that preach - ing tune __ For - tune, __ My Foe;

But this in bal - lads will sur - vive, I know,

Sung to that preach - ing tune, ___ For - tune, My Foe. ___

1. Fortune, my foe, why dost thou frown on me?
   And will thy favours never better be?
   Wilt thou, I say, forever breed my pain,
   And wilt thou not restore my joys again?
   Wilt thou, I say, forever breed my pain,
   And wilt thou not restore my joys again?

2. Fortune hath wrought me grief and great annoy;
   Fortune hath falsely stole my love away,
   My love and joy whose sight did make me glad;
   Such great misfortunes never young man had;
   My love and joy whose sight did make me glad;
   Such great misfortunes never young man had.

Additional verse from the book *Loyal Songs* written against the Rump Parliament, 1692, in the song "The Penitent Traytor":

> How could I bless thee, could'st thou take away
> My life and infamy both in one day?
> But this in ballads will survive I know,
> Sung to that preaching tune, Fortune, My Foe;
> But this in ballads will survive I know,
> Sung to that preaching tune, Fortune, My Foe.

As one of the best-known songs of the Elizabethan era, there are allusions to "Fortune, My Foe" in the plays of Shakespeare, Jonson, Beaumont, Fletcher, and others. Among composers who have made settings of the melody, besides Sweelinck, are Byrd, Scheidt, Ballet, Dowland, Tomkins, Haussman, Valerius, and many lesser names. Their arrangements were for virginal, harpsichord, lute, viola da gamba, or voices.

Through the broadsides that were hawked in the streets of cities and small towns, the people learned of the last lamentations of many a criminal about to be hanged. "Fortune, My Foe," through such notoriety, continued to be popular for some time.

The tune served other texts and was also printed under other names. As "Dr. Faustus" (printed in 1588–1589) it begins:

> All Christian men, give ear a whyle to me . . .

The opening line of "Titus Andronicus' Complaint," a ballad contemporary with Shakespeare's play, is,

> You noble minds and famous martial wights . . .

The following moralizing verse is from "Ayme Not Too Hie":

> Ayme not too hie in things above thy reach,
> Be not too foolish in thine own conceit;
> As thou hast wit and worldly wealth at will,
> So give Him thanks that shall increase it still.

As was the practice of the times, the variations consist of contrapuntal treatment of motifs from the melody, with increasingly florid passages in successive variations. Sweelinck shows great skill in his handling of imitation, especially effective with diminution of a motif.

2

GO FROM MY WINDOW

THOMAS MORLEY (1557–1603)

[Moderately]

1. Go from my win - dow, love, go. Go from my win - dow, my dear; The wind and the rain Will drive you back a - gain; You can - not be lodg - èd here.

MUSIC SOURCE: *Fitzwilliam Virginal Book;* reprint: Dover Publications, Inc.

Vocal line and text added by the editor. Text from William Chappell, *Old English Popular Music,* London, 1893.

2. Be - gone, be - gone, my jug - gy, my pug - gy, _____

Be - gone, my love, my dear; The

wea - ther is warm, 'Twill ___ do thee no ___ harm; Thou

canst not be lodg - èd here. _____

3. Go from my win - dow, my love, my love,

Go from my win - dow, my dear; For the

4. Come up to my win - dow, love, come, come,

1. Go from my window, love, go,
   Go from my window, my dear;
     The wind and the rain
     Will drive you back again;
   You cannot be lodgèd here.

2. Begone, begone, my juggy, my puggy,
   Begone, my love, my dear;
     The weather is warm,
     'Twill do thee no harm;
   Thou canst not be lodgèd here.

3. Go from my window, my love, my love,
   Go from my window, my dear;
     For the wind is in the west
     And the cuckoo's in his nest,
   And you canst not be lodgèd here.

4. Come up to my window, love, come, come, come,
   Come to my window, my dear;
     The wind nor the rain
     Shall trouble thee again;
   But thou shalt be lodgèd here.

other variants:

Go from my window, my love, my love,
Go from my window, my dear;
  The wind is blowing high
  And the ship is lying by,
So you cannot get a harb'ring here.

Go from my window, my love, my love,
Go from my window, my dear;
  The devil's in the man
  That he will not understan'
That he cannot get a harb'ring here.

"Go from My Window" is a tune that has been the theme of many settings by the English keyboard masters and lutenist composers, among them Byrd, Bull, Thomkins, Holborne, and Dowland. It is also found in several Dutch song books. In one of them it has the peculiar, perhaps phonetic, spelling "Gophromowinde Milort."

The text also has many variants. In religious garb, it goes like this:

Quho [*Who*] is at my windo? Quho, quho?
Go from my windo, go, go.
Quho callis thair, sa lyke a strainger?
Go from my windo, go.

Lord, I am heir, ane wretchit [*here, a wretched*] mortall,
That for thy mercy dois cry and call
Unto thee, my Lord celestiall
Se quho [*See who*] is at my windo, quho?

from: *Godly and Spiritual Songs*
(Edinburgh, 1590)

The version relating to the sailorman is printed with the song text.

The song stems from the pagan custom in which a young man is allowed secret entrance to the bedroom of his betrothed prior to marriage. The ritual required the youth to plead for admittance and the girl to be reluctant but finally to relent. The basic idea appeared in later times when it became the song of the married woman and illicit lover, who is warned that the husband is at home:

For the wind is in the west
And the cuckoo's [cuckold?] in his nest.

This theme and song are in Thomas Heywood's play *The Rape of Lucrece* (1608) and in *Frauncis New Iigge* (Jig), an Elizabethan song and dance entertainment with three stock characters: Frauncis, a gentleman; Richard, a farmer; and Besse, his wife.

3

THE MERRY WOOING OF ROBIN AND JOAN

(*Sellinger's Round*)

WILLIAM BYRD (1542?–1623)

[With a lilt, and with humor]

1. O moth - er, chave bin a batch - e - lour, ___ This twelve and twan - ty yeare; _____ And I'ze have of - ten beene a wow - ing, ___ And yet cham nev - er the neare: _____ Ione Grom - ball chee'l ___ ha'

2. (She) zaies if ize ___ cou'd daunce and zing, ___ As Thom - as Mil - ler con, _____ Or cut a cau - per, as lit - tle Iack Tay - lor, O how chee'd love ___ me thon. _____ But zoft and faire, ___ chil'

MUSIC SOURCE: *Fitzwilliam Virginal Book;* reprint: Dover Publications, Inc.

Vocal line and text added by the editor. Text from *Wit Restored* (1658). Widener Library, Harvard University.

ROBIN:

have thee try her once a-gaine, __ She can but say thee nay. _____ Then

O Gra-mar-cy moth - er, Chi'll zet a good vace o' the mat - ter, Chi'll

dresse up my zell' as fine as a dog And chi'll have a fresh bout __ at her.

4. And

in ———— my capp, ——Then oh how I'ch ———— shall swag-ger.

MOTHER:

5. Nay,

tak thee a lock - rum nap - kin son, ———— To wipe thy snot - ty

nose.

ROBIN:

T's noe mat - ter · vor that, ———— chi'll snort it out, ———— And

MOTHER:

vlurt it a - thart my cloths; Ods bod - kins, nay, fy a -

way,_____ I pre - thee son, do not so;_____ Be man - ner - ly, son, till

thou ___ canst tell, wheth - er sheele ha' thee or noe.

ROBIN:

6. But zir - rah, Moth - er, harke a - while, Whoes that that comes so

MOTHER:

near? 'Tis Ione Grum - ball, hold thy peace, __ For fear that she doe

ROBIN:

heare. Nay, on't be she, __ chi'll dresse my words In zuch a schol - ard's

grace, __ But virst __ of all chall take __ my honds And lay them a - thwart her

vace.

(to JOAN:)

7. Good mor - row, my hon - ey, my su - gar can - dy, My

lit - le pret - ty mouse, _____ Cha hopes thy va - ther and

moth - er be well, __ At home at thine own house. _____ I'ch

came vor love and I pray___ so tak't, Chi hopes che will not quar-rell.

JOAN:
9. O Rob - bin, dost thou love

ROBIN:
me so well? I vaith, a - bom - min - a - tion!_____

JOAN:
Why

10. Chave

land, chave houss, chave twa vat beasts, That's bet - ter thon vine speech-es.

JOAN:

T's a signe that For - tune fa - vours fooles, She lets them have such rich - es.

ROBIN:

Hark how she comes up-

on me now, I'd wish it be a good zine.

JOAN:

He that will steale an-y wit ___ from thee Had need to rise be-

time.

ROBIN

1. O Mother, chave bin a batchelour,   (... I've been ...)
   This twelve and twanty yeare;
   And I'ze have often beene a wowing,   (... I've often been wooing)
   And yet cham never the neare: (... I'm never the nearer)
   Ione Grumball chee'l ha' none a mee,   (... she'll have none of me)
   I'ze look so like a lowt;   (I look so like a lout)
   But I vaith, cham as propper a man as zhe, (... in faith, I am ... she)
   Zhe need not be zo stout.   (She ... so ...)

2. She zaies if I'ze cou'd daunce and zing,   (She says if I could dance and sing)
   As Thomas Miller con,   (... can)
   Or cut a cauper, as little Iack Taylor,   (... caper ...)
   O how chee'd love mee thon.   (... she'd love me then)
   But zoft and faire, chi'l none of that,   (But soft ..., I'll ...)
   I vaith cham not zo nimble;   (In faith, I'm ...)
   The Tailor hath nought to trouble his thought
   But his needel and his thimble.   (... needle ...)

MOTHER

3. O zon, th'art of a lawfull age,   (O son, ...)
   And a jolly tidy boy,
   I'de have thee try her once againe,
   She can but say thee nay.

ROBIN

   Then O Gramarcy mother,
   Chi'll zet a good vace o' the matter,   (I'll set a good face on ...)
   Chi'll dresse up my zel' as fine as a dog (... myself ...)
   And chi'll have a fresh bout at her.

4. And first chi'll put on my Zunday 'parrell (... Sunday apparel)
   That's lac't about the quarters;
   With a paire of buckram slopps,
   And a vlanting paire of garters.   (... flaunting ...)
   With my sword tide vast to my zide,   (... fast to my side)
   And my grandvather's dug'en and dagger,
   And a peacock's feather in my capp,
   Then oh how I'ch shall swagger.

MOTHER

5. Nay, tak thee a lockrum napkin, son,
   To wipe thy snotty nose,

ROBIN

   T's noe matter vor that, chi'll snort it out,
   And vlurt it athart my cloths: (And wipe it on my clothes)

MOTHER

Ods bodikins, nay, fy away,
I prethee, son, do not so:
Be mannerly, son, till thou canst tell
Whether sheele ha' thee or noe.

ROBIN

6. But zirrah, Mother, harke a while,
Whoes that that comes so neare?

MOTHER

'Tis Ione Grumball, hold thy peace,
For feare that she doe heare.

ROBIN

Nay, on't be she, chi'll dresse my words   *(. . . I'll address . . .)*
In zuch a scholard's grace,   *(In such a scholar's grace)*
But virst of all chall take my honds   *(. . . first . . . hands)*
And lay them athwart her vace.   *(. . . . face)*

ROBIN

7. Good morrow, my honey, my sugar candy,
My little pretty mouse,
Cha hopes thy vather and mother be well,   *(I . . . father . . .)*
At home at thine own house.
I'ch am zhame-vac't to show my mind,   *(I am shame-faced . . .)*
Cham sure thou knowst my arrant: *(I am . . . errand)*
Zome zain, Jugg, that I mun ha' thee.   *(Some're saying, dear, . . .*
    I must . . .)

JOAN

At leisure, Sir, I warrant.

8. "You must," Sir Clowne, is for the King,
And not for such a mon;   *(. . . man)*
You might have said, "by leave, faire maid,"
And let your "must" alone.

ROBIN

Ich am noe more a clowne, that's vlat,   *(. . . that's flat)*
Cham in my Zunday 'parrell,
I'ch came vor love and I pray so tak't,
Chi hopes che will not quarrell.

JOAN

9. O Robbin, dost thou love me so well?

ROBIN

I vaith, abommination!

JOAN

Why then, you should have fram'd your words
Into a finer fashion.

ROBIN

Vine vashions and vine speeches too (*Fine fashions and fine . . .*)
As schollards volks can utter, (. . . *scholar folks . . .*)
Chad wrather speak but twa words plaine (*I'd rather . . . two words . . .*)
Than haulfe a score and stutter. (*Than half a score . . .*)

10. Chave land, chave houss, chave twa vat beasts, (*I have . . . fat . . .*)
That's better thon vine speeches.

JOAN

T's a signe that Fortune favours fooles
She lets them have such riches.

ROBIN

Hark how she comes upon mee now,
I'd wish it be a good zine. (. . . *good sign*)

JOAN

He that will steale any wit from thee
Had need to rise betime.

"Sellinger's Round," or "The Beginning of the World," was a very popular six-teenth-century dance tune. Its popularity is attested to by many literary references in works by Jonson, Fletcher, Heywood, Devanant, and Morley. A colorful de-scription of the dance scene is in *Bacchus Bountie* (1593): "While thus they tip-pled, the fiddler he fiddled, and the pots danced for joy the old hop-about commonly called 'Sellinger's Round.'" The "round" here is not to be confused with vocal rounds that are sung canonically or in imitation. It is derived from the circle forma-tion in "round" dances in contrast to the parallel lines or squares of other country dances.

"The Merry Wooing of Robin and Joan," one among other texts that have been set to the tune, was printed in *Wit and Drollery* (1682) and in *Wit Re-stored* (1658). Its inclusion in these collections, Baskervill suggests in *The Eliza-bethan Jig* (1929), indicates that it was intended as a farce for the audience of the court. The clown's dialect (Robin) is entertainment catering to the demands of the courtiers for burlesque of the countryman or yeoman. In the dialect of this song, the "ch" should be guttural as in the German "ich."

The ornamentation in the *Fitzwilliam Virginal Book* was indicated by the signs:

. According to one authority on this subject, Edward Dannreuther, their execution should be as follows:

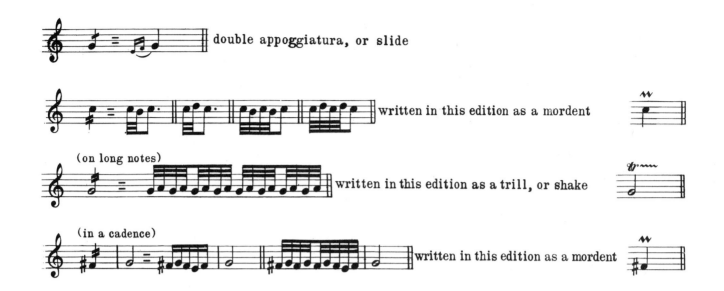

double appoggiatura, or slide

written in this edition as a mordent

(on long notes)

written in this edition as a trill, or shake

(in a cadence)

written in this edition as a mordent

Of course, these ornaments are subject to individual interpretation, depending upon the musical context.

4

HARVEST HOME

JOHN DRYDEN (1631–1700)   HENRY PURCELL (1659–1695)

1. Your hay it is mow'd and your corn ____ is reap'd, Your barns will be full and your hov-els heap'd. Come, boys, come, Come, boys, come; And mer-ri-ly roar out our har-vest home!

2. We've cheat-ed the par-son, we'll cheat him a-gain, For why should a block-head have one in ten? One in ten, One in ten, For why should a block-head have one in ten?

CHORUS

Har-vest home, Har-vest home, And mer-ri-ly roar out our har-vest home!

MUSIC AND TEXT SOURCE: *King Arthur* by H. Purcell.

1. Your hay it is mow'd and your corn is reap'd,
   Your barns will be full and your hovels heap'd.
      Come, boys, come,
      Come, boys, come,
   And merrily roar out our harvest home!

CHORUS: Harvest home,
            Harvest home,
   And merrily roar out our harvest home!

2. We've cheated the parson, we'll cheat him again,
   For why should a blockhead have one in ten?
      One in ten,
      One in ten,
   For why should a blockhead have one in ten?

3. For prating so long, like a book-learnt sot,
   Till pudding and dumpling are burnt to th' pot;
      Burnt to th' pot,
      Burnt to th' pot,
   Till pudding and dumpling are burnt to th' pot.

4. We'll toss off our ale till we cannot stand,
   And heigh for the honour of old England;
      Old England,
      Old England,
   And heigh for the honour of old England.

Henry Purcell wrote many works for the Restoration theater. In the last five years of his short life—thirty-six years—he composed incidental music for forty plays as well as four opera-spectacles. *King Arthur,* written in 1691 in collaboration with John Dryden, was one of his most successful operas. It contains the song "Harvest Home." In the preface to the opera, Dryden set forth the problems of the librettist:

There is nothing better than what I intended, but the music . . . through the artful hands of Mr. Purcel [*sic*] who has compos'd it with so great a genius. . . . But the Numbers of Poetry and Vocal Musick are sometimes so contrary, that in many places I have been obliged to cramp my Verses, and make them rugged to the Reader, that they may be harmonious to the Hearer. Of which I have no Reason to repent me, because these sorts of Entertainment are principally for the Ear and Eye.

"Harvest Home" is sung in the Finale (Act V, Scene ii) by Comus and three peasants. The composer's manuscript has been lost, but there is a manuscript copy in the British Museum, dated 1704. A slightly varied version is found in D'Urfey's song collection *Wit and Mirth* (1719–1720). In the ballad opera *Polly* (1729), by John Gay and John Christopher Pepusch, the tune is further varied.

5

SALLY IN OUR ALLEY

HENRY CAREY (1685–1743)   LUDWIG VAN BEETHOVEN (1770–1827)

Andantino grazioso semplice

Of all the girls____ that are so smart,____ There's none like pret - ty Sal - ly! She is the dar - ling___ of my heart,____ And she lives in our al - ley. There's not a la - dy

MUSIC AND TEXT SOURCE: G. Thomson; also *Beethoven's Werke,* Breitkopf and Härtel.

in the land   That's half so sweet ___ as ___ Sal - ly;   She

rit.   *a tempo*

is the dar - ling   of my heart, ___   And she lives in ___ our ___ al - ley.

rit.   *a tempo*

last time only

1. Of all the girls that are so smart,
   There's none like pretty Sally!
   She is the darling of my heart,
   And she lives in our alley.
   There's not a lady in the land
   That's half so sweet as Sally;
   She is the darling of my heart,
   And she lives in our alley.

2. Her father he makes cabbage nets,
   And thro' the streets doth cry 'em;
   Her mother she sells laces long
   To such as please to buy 'em;
   But sure such folk could ne'er beget
   So sweet a girl as Sally;
   She is the darling of my heart,
   And she lives in our alley.

3. When she is by, I leave my work,
   I love her so sincerely;
   My master comes, like any Turk,
   And bangs me most severely;
   But let him bang, long as he will,
   I'll bear it all for Sally;
   She is the darling of my heart,
   And she lives in our ally.

4. Of all the days in the week,
   I dearly love but one day,
   And that's the day that comes betwixt
   A Saturday and Monday;
   For then I'm drest in all my best
   To walk abroad with Sally;
   She is the darling of my heart,
   And she lives in our ally.

5. My master carries me to church
   And often I am blamed
   Because I leave him in the lurch,
   Soon as the text is named;
   I leave the church in sermon time,
   And slink away to Sally;
   She is the darling of my heart,
   And she lives in our alley.

6. When Christmas comes about again,
   Oh then I shall have money;
   I'll board it up and box it all,
   And give it to my honey;
   And would it were a thousand pounds,
   I'd give it all to Sally;
   She is the darling of my heart,
   And she lives in our alley.

7. My master and the neighbors all
   Make game of me and Sally,
   And but for her I'd better be
   A slave and row a galley;
   But when my seven long years are out,
   Oh then I'll marry Sally;
   She is the darling of my heart,
   And she lives in our alley.

Henry Carey was a composer as well as a dramatist and a poet. He had composed his own music to the above verses, but about 1760, his melody was superseded by another tune, "The Country Lass," which was adapted to Carey's verses, and is the one Beethoven wrote this setting for.

Carey writes about the genesis of his song thus:

A shoemaker's 'prentice, making holiday with his sweetheart, treated her with a sight of Bedlam, the puppet shows, the flying chairs, and all the elegancies of Moorfields, from whence proceeding to the farthing-pye house, he gave her a collection of buns, cheese-cakes, gammon of bacon, stuffed beef and bottled ale, through all which scenes the author dodged them. Charmed with the simplicity of their courtship, he drew from what he witnessed this little sketch of nature; but being then young and obscure, he was very much ridiculed by some of his acquaintance for this performance, which nevertheless made its way into the polite world and amply recompensed him by the applause of the divine Addison,* who was pleased more than once to mention it with approbation.

There were many parodies of Carey's original tune, among them "Sally in Our Alley to Billy in Piccadilly" and "Sally Rivall'd by Country Molly." The tune now current was widely used in plays and ballad operas, notably *The Beggar's Opera* (1728).

---

* Joseph Addison (1672–1719), essayist, poet, statesman, co-publisher and contributor to the periodical *The Spectator*.

6

THE MILLER OF DEE
(*The Budgeon*)

LUDWIG VAN BEETHOVEN (1770–1827)

Allegretto con brio

There was a jol - ly mill - er once Lived
I love my mill,— she is to me Like

on — the riv - er Dee; He worked— and sang— from—
par - ent, child — and wife; I would— not change— my—

morn — till night, No lark— more blythe— than he. And —
sta - tion For an - y oth - er in life. Then —

MUSIC AND TEXT SOURCE: G. Thomson; also *Beethoven's Werke*, Breitkopf and Härtel.

this the bur - den of his song For - ev - er used to be: _____ I
push, push, push the bowl, my boys, And pass_ it 'round to me; _____ The

care _ for no - bod-y, no, _ not I, If _ no - bod-y cares _ for me. _____
long - er we _ sit here _ and drink, The _ mer - ri - er we _ shall be. _____

1. 2.   3.

1. There was a jolly miller once
   Lived on the river Dee;
   He worked and sang from morn till night,
   No lark more blythe than he.
   And this the burden of his song
   Forever used to be:
   I care for nobody, no, not I,
   If nobody cares for me.

2. I love my mill, she is to me
   Like parent, child and wife;
   I would not change my station
   For any other in life.
   Then push, push, push the bowl, my boys,
   And pass it 'round to me;
   The longer we sit here and drink,
   The merrier we shall be.

3. So let us his example take,
   And be from malice free;
   Let everyone his neighbor serve,
   As served he'd like to be.
   And merrily push the can about,
   And drink and sing with glee:
   If nobody cares a doit for us,
   Why, not a doit care we.

THE BUDGEON IT IS A DELICATE TRADE

The budgeon it is a delicate trade,
And a delicate trade of fame;
For when that we have bit the bloe,
We carry away the game.
But if the cully nab us, and
The lurries from us take,
O then he rubs us to the whit,
Though we are not worth a make.

"The Miller of Dee" appeared in the ballad opera *Love in a Village* in 1762, but the tune is found as early as 1674 to the words of "The Budgeon." The "budgeon" is the delicate trade of burglary where the door of a house is opened slightly and articles near the door are stolen. Perhaps the name is derived from an article of clothing, a "budge"—a lambskin coat with sheep's wool on the outside. Beethoven's droning ostinato bass in the introduction and interludes evokes the sound of a busy mill and the bouncing accompaniment keeps the miller jolly.

The version by Beethoven in Thomson and the one in Chappell's *Old English Popular Music* are in the minor key. Here is the same tune in the Aeolian mode with the lowered seventh (F♮), as notated from the singing of a peasant by Vaughan Williams:

7

SALISBURY PLAIN

RALPH VAUGHAN WILLIAMS (1872–1958)

1. As I walked o-ver Salis-bu-ry Plain, Oh,—
there I met a scamp-ing— young blade. He— kissed me and en-
tic-ed me so,— Till a-long with him I was forced— for to go.

Variant

1. As I walked over Salisbury Plain,
   Oh, there I met a scamping young blade.
   He kissed me and enticed me so,
   Till along with him I was forced for to go.

2. We came unto a public house at last,
   And there for man and wife we did pass.
   He called for ale and wine and strong beer,
   Till at length we both to bed did repair.

3. "Undress yourself, my darling," says he,
   "Undress yourself, and come to bed with me."
   "Oh yes, that I will," then says she,
   "If you'll keep all those flash girls away."

4. "Those flash girls you need not fear,
   For you'll be safe-guarded, my dear.
   I'll maintain you as some lady so gay,
   For I'll go a-robbing on the highway."

5. Early next morning my love he arose,
   And so nimbly he put on his clothes.
   Straight to the highway he set sail,
   And 'twas there he robbed the coaches of the mail.

6. Oh, it's now my love in Newgate Jail do lie,
   Expecting every moment to die.
   The Lord have mercy on his poor soul,
   For I think I hear the death-bell for to toll.

The highwayman's "goodnight" ballad, in which the hero turns robber to support his wife and ends up on the gallows, was a favorite with eighteenth- and nineteenth-century fairground singers and balladmongers. Such ballads were usually announced as "the dying testament" of some well-known thief. The present song gains piquancy through being put in the mouth of the robber's sweetheart.

8

THE BASKET OF EGGS

RALPH VAUGHAN WILLIAMS (1872–1958)

[Rhythmically]

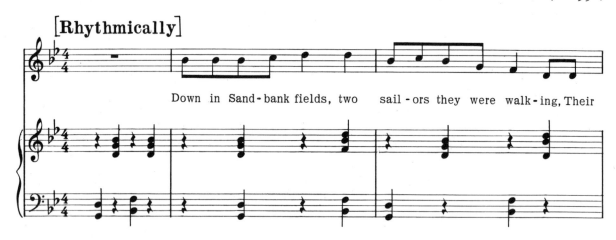

Down in Sand-bank fields, two sail-ors they were walk-ing, Their

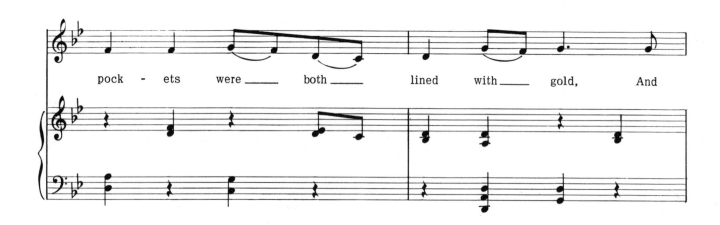

pock - ets were ____ both ____ lined with ____ gold, And

as to-geth - er they ___ were ___ talk - ing, A fair maid there ___ they ___

did be - hold, With a lit - tle bas - ket

stand - ing __ by her, As she sat down to take her __ ease. To

car - ry it for her one of them __ of - fered. The an - swer was: __ "Sir, __

1. — 5.

6.

if you __ please." _____

1. Down in Sandbank fields, two sailors they were walking,
   Their pockets were both lined with gold,
   And as together they were talking,
   A fair maid there they did behold,
   With a little basket standing by her,
   As she sat down to take her ease.
   To carry it for her one of them offered.
   The answer was: "Sir, if you please."

2. One of these sailors took the basket.
   "There's eggs in the basket, please take care;
   And if by chance you should out-walk me,
   At the Half-way House please leave them there."
   Behold, these sailors, they did outwalk her,
   The Half-way House they did pass by.
   This pretty damsel she laughed at their fancy,
   And on the sailors she kept her eye.

3. When these two sailors came unto an ale-house,
   There they did call for a pint of wine,
   Saying: "Landlord, landlord, what fools in this nation!
   This young maid from her eggs we've twined.
   O landlord, landlord, bring us some bacon.
   We have got these eggs and we'll have some dressed."
   Behold, these sailors were much mistaken,
   As you shall say when you hear the rest.

4. 'Twas then the landlord he went to the basket,
   Expecting of some eggs to find.
   He said: "Young man, you're much mistaken,
   Instead of eggs I've found a child."
   Then one of them sat down to weeping.
   The other one said: "It's not worth while.
   Here's fifty guineas I'll give to the baby,
   If any woman will take the child."

5. The pretty young damsel she sat by the fire,
   And she had a shawl drawn over her face.
   She said: "I'll take it and kindly use it,
   When first I see the money paid."
   One of the sailors threw down the money.
   Great favour to the babe was shown.
   "Since it is so, then let's be friendly,
   For you know, this child is yours and mine.

6. "Don't you remember a-dancing with Nancy,
   As long ago as Easter day?"
   "Oh yes, and I do, and she pleased my fancy,
   So now the fiddler I have paid."
   One of the sailors went up to the basket,
   And he kicked the basket over and o'er.
   "Since it is so, may we all be contented,
   But I'm hanged if I'll like eggs any more."

The theme of the girl with a basket in which is concealed an unwanted child is a recurrent one in farces and "jigs" of the seventeenth century. In these, she generally outwits the lustful lover. In Thomas Jordan's *Cheaters Cheated* (1664), Mol sings to Wat, a country bumpkin (from Baskervill, *The Elizabethan Jig*):

> If thou wilt dance, then I will sing
> And thou shalt bear the burden.*

After awhile:

> But I have too much strain'd my throat,
> I prethe sing a little.

She dances off, leaving Wat dancing, singing, and holding the basket. When he looks behind him and does not see Mol, he sings:

> But yvaith if zhe be gon   (. . . *in faith, if she be gone*)
> Ich chill keep her basket.   (*I shall* . . .)

He then discovers the infant. Eventually he manages to have the basket stolen from him by two rogues whom he dupes into thinking it is filled with treasures.

In Middleton's play *Chaste Maid in Cheapside* (1630), the child in a basket is covered with meat. In a song from Tiersot's *Chansons populaires recueillés dans les Alpes françaises,* a basket full of bread conceals the child.

---

* Burden has a double meaning here, also referring to the refrain of a tune.

9

THE FOGGY, FOGGY DEW

BENJAMIN BRITTEN (1913–)

ev - er did wrong, was to woo a fair young maid. I
on ____ my bed ____ and she be - gan to weep. She

espress.

poco più f

wooed her in the win - ter time, and in the sum - mer
sighed, she cried, she damn near died, she said: What shall I

poco più f

too. ____ And the on - ly, on - ly thing ____ I did ____ that was wrong, was to
do? ____ So I hauled her in - to bed and I cover - ed up her head, just to

p

pp

1. 2.   ‖ **3.** *dying away* *ppp*

keep her from the fog - gy, fog - gy dew.   2. One   dew. ____
keep her from the fog - gy, fog - gy dew.   3. Oh

ppp

1. When I was a bachelor I lived all alone,
   and worked at the weaver's trade,
   And the only, only thing that I ever did wrong,
   was to woo a fair young maid.
   I wooed her in the winter time,
   and in the summer too . . .
   And the only, only thing I did that was wrong,
   was to keep her from the foggy, foggy dew.

2. One night she came to my bedside
   when I lay fast asleep;
   She laid her head upon my bed
   and she began to weep.
   She sighed, she cried, she damn near died,
   she said: What shall I do? . . .
   So I hauled her into bed and I covered up her head,
   just to keep her from the foggy, foggy dew.

3. Oh I am a bachelor and I live with my son,
   and we work at the weaver's trade.
   And ev'ry single time that I look into his eyes,
   he reminds me of the fair young maid.
   He reminds me of the winter time,
   and of the summer too, . . .
   And of the many, many times that I held her in my arms,
   just to keep her from the foggy, foggy dew . . .

The phrase, "the foggy dew," also appears in a quite well-known but different ballad, an Irish folk song in the minor mode. The song from Suffolk that Benjamin Britten has arranged is in a major key. In what seems like a traditional treatment, there are subtle, unusual touches in the harmony and the doubling and syncopating of the melody in the bass. Britten has made many settings of folk songs of the British Isles and France and they all bear the imprint of his unique treatment and skilled craftsmanship. He has performed them in recitals throughout the concert world with the singer Peter Pears. The magazine *Punch* once commented on this team:

There's no need for Pears
To give himself airs;
He has them written
By Benjamin Britten.

II

IRISH SONGS

Rᴇꜰᴇʀᴇɴᴄᴇs to Irish music go back to medieval times. Pictures of the harp engraved on coins from the reign of King John (1185–1216) have been found in Ireland. The poetry of the early bards has been preserved in manuscripts, but not the tunes they chanted or their harp music. Nothing remains of the early music except the folk songs that may have been preserved through oral tradition. The first notation of the tunes occurred when "Callinoo Casturame," a corruption of "Cailín ó chois tSiúire mé" ("I am a girl from beside the Suir"), was included in a tablature manuscript collection, William Ballet's Lute Book (circa 1600).

When English increasingly became the language of the British Isles, it was set to airs formerly sung with Irish words. These new texts were printed on broadsides that were eagerly bought up in the towns and at the markets and fairs in the countryside. The content of these broadsides was the topical songs of the day. But among the new songs were those with patriotic texts, such as "The Wearing o' the Green" and "The Croppy Boy."

Another more lyric type of Irish folk song in English were those for which Thomas Moore (1779–1852) wrote the poems. It is through his texts in *Irish*

Melodies that a great many songs of Erin have become known. His poetry, however, has been criticized by a number of scholars. Patrick Galvin writes: "As he himself admitted in a moment of insight, in the song so aptly and wistfully entitled 'O Blame Not the Bard,' what he did was to offer his country's oppressors an inoffensive and genteel portrayal of her sufferings, to the end that 'The masters themselves, as they rivet thy chains,/Shall pause at the song of their captive and weep!' "* Hazlitt said that Moore had "converted the wild harp of Erin into a musical snuff-box." Sparling declared that Moore "had tinkered most of the old tunes he used into drawing-room shapes." And yet, Galvin admits that many airs are exquisite, memorable, beautiful, suited to the music room or recital hall.

* Patrick Galvin, *Irish Songs of Resistance,* The Folklore Press, N.Y.C.

10

LILLIBURLERO

HENRY PURCELL (1659–1695)

MUSIC SOURCE: *Lesson* for the harpsichord, "A new Irish tune."
Vocal line and text added by the editor.

1. Ho! broder Teague, dost hear de decree?   (. . . *brother Teague* . . .)
        Lilliburlero bullen a la.
     Dat we shall have a new deputie?
        Lilliburlero bullen a la.
        Lero, lero, lilliburlero,
     Lero, lero, bullen a la,
        Lero, lero, lilliburlero,
        Lero, lero bullen a la.

2. Ho! by Shaint Tyburn, it is de Talbot,   (. . . *by Saint Tyburn*)
        Lilliburlero (etc.)
     And he will cut all de English troat.
        Lilliburlero (etc.)

3. Tho' by my shoul de English do praat,   (. . . *by my soul . . . prattle*)
     De laws on dare side, and Creish knows what.   (. . . *their side, and Christ* . . .)

4. But if dispence do come from de pope,   (. . . *dispensation* . . .)
     We'll hang Magna Charta and dem in a rope.

5. For de good Talbot is made a lord,
     And with brave lads is coming aboard:

6. Who all in France have taken a sware   (. . . *swear*)
     Dat dey will have no Protestant heir.

7. Ara! but why does he stay behind?
     Ho! by my shoul 'tis a Protestant wind.

8. But see, de Tyrconnel is now coming ashore,
     And we shall have commissions galore.

9. And he dat will not go to mass
     Shall be turn out, and look like an ass.

10. But now de hereticks all go down,
     By Creish and Shaint Patrick, de nation's our own.

11. Dare was an old prophecy found in a bog,
     "Ireland shall be rul'd by an ass and a dog."

12. And now dis prophecy is come to pass,
     For Talbot's de dog and James is de ass.

First printed in *The Delightful Companion* (1686), the song was described as follows in Bishop Gilbert Burnet's *History of His own Times* (1723–1734):

A foolish ballad was made at that time, treating the Papists, and chiefly the Irish, in a very ridiculous manner, which had a burden, said to be Irish words, "Lero, lero, lilliburlero," that made an impression on the [King's] army, that cannot be imagined by those who saw it not. The whole army, and at last the people, both in city and country, were singing it perpetually. And, perhaps, never had so slight a thing so great an effect.

William Stenhouse, in his notes for *Scots Musical Museum,* claims that "lilliburlero" and "bullen-a-lah" were passwords used by the Irish papists in their massacre of the Protestants in 1641.

The work for harpsichord "A new Irish tune" was listed as "by Mr. Purcell" in *Musick's Handmaid* (1689). There are many other texts sung to the tune, the best known of which is "The Protestant Boys." Purcell also used the melody as a bass for a jig in his stage-work *The Gordian Knot Unty'd* (1691):

Lilliburlero in bass (*8va lower*)..

loco

59

11

OH! WHO MY DEAR DERMOT

(*Avenging and Bright*)

WILLIAM SMYTH (c. 1800)   LUDWIG VAN BEETHOVEN (1770–1827)

Andante con espressione

1. Oh! who, my dear Dermot, has dared to deceive thee, And what's the dishonour this gold is to buy? Back, And
2. Tho' poor, we are honest, and will this not cheer us, Thy sire and thy grandsire have asked for no more. And

MUSIC AND TEXT SOURCE: G. Thomson, also *Beethoven's Werke,* Breitkopf and Härtel.

back to thy tempt - er, or No - rah shall leave thee, To
shame with its shad - ow has nev - er come near us To

hide her in woods and in des - arts to
shut out the sun from our cab - in be -

1. 2. 3.   4.

die.
fore.

1. Oh! who, my dear Dermot, has dared to deceive thee,
   And what's the dishonour this gold is to buy?
   Back, back to thy tempter, or Norah shall leave thee,
   To hide her in woods, and in desarts to die.

2. Tho' poor, we are honest, and will this not cheer us,
   Thy sire and thy grandsire have asked for no more.
   And shame with its shadow has never come near us
   To shut out the sun from our cabin before.

3. Oh look at yon lark where the sky shines so brightly,
   Say why does it carol its echoing lay?
   Is't singing so gaily and mounting so lightly
   Because it finds gold in the dawn of the day?

4. Oh! Dermot, thy heart is with agony swelling,
   For, once it was honest and honour its law.
   An Irishman thou, and have bribes in thy dwelling!
   Back, back to thy tempter, go Erin go Bragh!

AVENGING AND BRIGHT

THOMAS MOORE

1. Avenging and bright fall the swift sword of Erin
   On him who the brave sons of Usna betray'd!
   For ev'ry fond eye he hath waken'd a tear in,
   A drop from his heart-wounds shall weep oe'r her blade!

2. By the red cloud that hung over Conor's dark dwelling,
   When Ulad's three champions lay sleeping in gore—
   By the billows of war, which so often high swelling,
   Have wafted these heroes to victory's shore.

3. We swear to revenge them!—no joy shall be tasted,
   The harp shall be silent, and the maiden unwed,
   Our halls shall be mute and our fields shall lie wasted,
   Till vengeance is wreak'd on the murderer's head!

4. Yes, monarch! tho' sweet are our home recollections,
   Tho' sweet are the tears that from tenderness fall,
   Tho' sweet are our friendships, our hopes, our affections,
   Revenge on a tyrant is sweetest of all!

The Thomson collection refers to the tune as "Crooghan a venne," but more correctly it is "Cruachan na Feine," *i.e.,* the Mountain of Finn, which was named after Finn MacCool of early Irish history. Moore's poem is founded on one of the oldest of Gaelic legends, "Dierdre, or the lamentable fate of the sons of Usna." A brief synopsis of the involved story follows:

At the birth of Dierdre, a Druid named Cathbad prophesied misfortune and doom for her——

> Child of sorrow, sin and shame,
> Dierdre be thy dreaded name!
> Child of doom, thy fatal charms
> Soon shall work us deadly harms.
>
> Long shall Ulster mourn the night
> Gave thine eyes their blasting light;
> Long shall Usnach rue the day
> Shew'd his sons their fatal ray!

As a beautiful woman, Dierdre became the object of rivalry between the King of Ulster and her lover Noisi. This resulted in her exile, recapture, and suicide, which was followed by a devastating war against Ulster, or Ulad, its ancient name, as it is called in the second verse.

12

THE PULSE OF AN IRISHMAN

(*Air: St. Patrick's Day*)   (*Though Dark Are Our Sorrows*)

ALEXANDER BOSWELL (1775–1822)   LUDWIG VAN BEETHOVEN (1770–1827)

Vivace scherzando

1. The pulse of an I - rish - man ev - er beats quick - er, When
2. Oh, blest be the land in the wide west - ern wa - ters, Sweet

war is the sto - ry, or love is the theme; And
E - rin, lov'd E - rin, the pride of my song; Still

MUSIC AND TEXT SOURCE: G. Thomson; also *Beethoven's Werke*, Breitkopf and Härtel.

No - rah, my jew - el, Is kind, and with smil - ing, All
dark - ling con - fu - sion, Like mists from the riv - er, Shall

sor - row be - guil - ing, Shall bid from our cab - in all
van - ish for - ev - er, And true I - rish hearts with warm

care to be gone; And how they will jig it, And
loy - al - ty glow; And proud ex - ul - ta - tion Burst

tug at the spi - got, On Pat - rick's day in the morn - ing."
forth from the na - tion On Pat - rick's day in the morn - ing.

1. The pulse of an Irishman ever beats quicker,
   When war is the story, or love is the theme;
   And place him where bullets fly thicker and thicker,
   You'll find him all cowardice scorning.
   And tho' a ball should maim poor Darby,
   Light at the heart he rallies on:
   "Fortune is cruel,
   But Norah, my jewel,
   Is kind, and with smiling,
   All sorrow beguiling,
   Shall bid from our cabin all care to be gone;
   And how they will jig it,
   And tug at the spigot,
   On Patrick's day in the morning."

2. Oh, blest be the land in the wide western waters,
   Sweet Erin, lov'd Erin, the pride of my song;
   Still brave be the sons, and still fair be the daughters
   Thy meads and thy mountains adorning!
   And tho' the eastern sun seems tardy,
   Tho' the pure light of knowledge slow,
   Night and delusion
   And darkling confusion,
   Like mists from the river,
   Shall vanish forever,
   And true Irish hearts with warm loyalty glow;
   And proud exultation
   Burst forth from the nation
   On Patrick's day in the morning.

THOUGH DARK ARE OUR SORROWS

THOMAS MOORE

1. Tho' dark are our sorrows, today we'll forget them
   And smile thro' our tears, like a sunbeam in show'rs;
   There never were hearts, if our rulers would let them,
   More form'd to be tranquil and blest than ours!
   But just when the chain
   Has ceased to pain,
   And hope has enwreath'd it round with flow'rs,
   There comes a new link
   Our spirit to sink!
   Oh! the joy that we taste, like the light of the poles,
   Is a flash amid darkness, too brilliant to stay;
   But tho' 'twere the last little spark in our souls,
   We must light it up now, on our Prince's Day.

2. Contempt on the minion who calls you disloyal!
   Tho' fierce to your foe, to your friends you are true;
   And the tribute most high to a head that is royal,
   Is love from a heart that loves liberty too.
   While cowards, who blight
   Your fame, your right,
   Would shrink from the blaze of the battle array,
   The standard of green
   In front would be seen—
   Oh, my life on your faith! were you summon'd this minute,
   You'd cast ev'ry bitter remembrance away,
   And show what the arm of old Erin has in it,
   When roused by the foe, on her Prince's Day.

3. He loves the Green Isle, and his love is recorded
   In hearts which have suffer'd too much to forget:
   And hope shall be crown'd and attachment rewarded,
   And Erin's gay jubilee shine out yet.
   The gem may be broke
   By many a stroke,
   But nothing can cloud its native ray,
   Each fragment will cast
   A light to the last.—
   And thus Erin, my country, tho' broken thou art,
   There's a lustre within thee that ne'er will decay;
   A spirit which beams thro' each suffering part,
   And now smiles at all pain on the Prince's Day.

The texts of both poems are sung to the well-known Irish dance tune "St. Patrick's Day." Alexander Boswell (1775–1822), poet and conservative Member of Parliament, sets forth in his patronizing verses a stereotype devil-may-care, fighting, drinking Irishman. Moore (1779–1852), on the other hand, describes the long-suffering and oppressed Irish who, nevertheless, on St. Patrick's Day give vent to their natural joy and ebullience. Ironically, the more revolutionary Irish considered Moore too conciliatory to the English in politics and in the content of his poems and too refined in his version of the melodies.

Beethoven also composed a set of variations on this tune, called erroneously *Air Ecossais,* no. 4 in *Ten Varied Themes for Piano Alone, or with Flute or Violin,* op. 107.

13

THE SOLDIER
(*The Minstrel Boy*)

WILLIAM SMYTH (C. 1800)   LUDWIG VAN BEETHOVEN (1770–1827)

Then sol - diers come fill high the wine, For we reck not of to - mor - row; Be ours to-day and we re-sign All the

'Tis you, 'tis I that may meet the ball; And me it bet - ter plea - ses In bat - tle, brave with the brave to fall, Than to

MUSIC AND TEXT SOURCE: G. Thomson; also *Beethoven's Werke*, Breitkopf and Härtel.

1. Then soldiers come fill high the wine,
   For we reck not of tomorrow;
   Be ours today and we resign
   All the rest to the fools of sorrow.
   Gay be the hour till we beat to arms;
   Then come rude Death or Glory;
   'Tis Victory in all her charms
   Or to Fame in the world's bright story.

2. 'Tis you, 'tis I that may meet the ball;
   And me it better pleases
   In battle, brave with the brave to fall,
   Than to die of dull diseases
   Driv'ller to be in my fireside chair
   With saws and tales unheeded
   A tott'ring thing of aches and cares,
   No longer loved nor needed.

3. But thou, oh dark is thy flowing hair,
   And thine eye with fire is streaming;
   And o'er thy cheek, thy looks, thine air
   Sits health in triumph beaming.
   Thou, brother soldier, fill the wine,
   Fill high to love and beauty;
   Love, friendship, honour, all are thine,
   Thy country and thy duty.

THE MINSTREL BOY

THOMAS MOORE

1. The minstrel boy to the war is gone,
   In the ranks of death you'll find him;
   His father's sword has he girded on,
   And his wild harp slung behind him.
   "Land of song!" said the warrior bard,
   "Though all the world betrays thee,
   One sword, at least, thy rights shall guard,
   One faithful harp shall praise thee!"

2. The minstrel fell!—but the foeman's chain
   Could not bring that proud soul under;
   The harp he loved ne'er spoke again,
   For he tore its chords asunder;
   And said, "No chains shall sully thee,
   Thou soul of love and bravery!
   Thy songs were made for the pure and free,
   They shall never sound in slavery."

The viewpoints of the English and Irish poets are at variance in their treatment of the Irish soldier. The former urges upon the soldier a cavalier attitude toward life, and loyalty to the British empire:

> . . . "honour, are thine,
> Thy country and thy duty"

whereas Moore emphasizes the tragic and heroic struggle of the Irish for freedom. Apparently George Thomson, in editing Smyth's four-stanza poem, compressed the first two stanzas into one. Significantly, the Scotsman Thomson changed the original line, "Or fame in Britain's story," to "Or to fame in the world's bright story."

Since the Beethoven setting is to the poem by Smyth, it has a martial character that is underscored by drum effects, open octaves, and sparse harmony—quite different from the expressive chordal accompaniments to which we are accustomed.

14

'TIS THE LAST ROSE OF SUMMER

(The Groves of Blarney)

THOMAS MOORE (1779–1852)   FELIX MENDELSSOHN (1809–1847)

'Tis the last rose of __ sum-mer, Left __ bloom - ing __ a - lone; All her love-ly __ com - pan - ions Are __ fad - ed __ and __ gone; No __ flow'r of her kin - dred, No __ rose - bud __ is

MUSIC SOURCE: *Fantasie sur une chanson Irlandaise,* Op. 15 (excerpt). Vocal line and text added by the editor.

nigh   To re - flect back her __ blush - es,   Or __ give __ sigh _ for _ sigh.

f   *dim.*   *p*   *poco rit.*

1. 'Tis the last rose of summer,
   Left blooming alone;
   All her lovely companions
   Are faded and gone;
   No flow'r of her kindred,
   No rosebud is nigh
   To reflect back her blushes,
   Or give sigh for sigh.

2. I'll not leave thee, thou lone one,
   To pine on the stem;
   Since the lovely are sleeping,
   Go sleep thou with them;
   Thus kindly I scatter
   Thy leaves o'er the bed,
   Where thy mates of the garden
   Lie scentless and dead.

3. So soon may I follow,
   When friendships decay,
   And from love's shining circle
   The gems drop away!
   When true hearts lie wither'd
   And fond ones are flown,
   Oh! who would inhabit
   This bleak world alone?

THE GROVES OF BLARNEY

1. The groves of Blarney, they are so charming,
   All by the purling of sweet silent streams,
   Being bank'd with posies that spontaneous grow there,
   Planted in order by the sweet rock close:
   'Tis there the daisy and the sweet carnation,
   The blooming pink and the rose so fair, . . .
   The daffy-down-dilly, beside the lily,
   Flow'rs that scent the sweet fragrant air.

2. 'Tis Lady Jeffreys that owns this station,
   Like Alexander or Queen Helen fair,
   There's no commander throughout the nation,
   For emulation can with her compare:
   She has castles round her that no nine-pounder
   Could dare to plunder her place of strength;
   But Oliver Cromwell, he did her pummel,
   And made a breach in her battlement.

3. There's gravel walks there for speculation,
   And conversation in sweet solitude;
   'Tis there the lover may hear the dove, or
   The gentle plover in the afternoon,
   And if a young lady should be so engaging
   As to walk alone in those shady bow'rs,
   'Tis there her courtier he may transport her
   In some dark fort or underground.

4. For 'tis there the cave where no daylight enters,
   But bats and badgers are forever bred;
   Being moss'd by nature, that makes it sweeter
   Than a coach and six or a feather bed.
   'Tis there the lake that is stor'd with perches
   And comely eels in the verdant mud, . . .
   Beside the leeches and the groves of beeches,
   All standing in order to guard the flood.

5. 'Tis there the kitchen hangs many a flitch in,
   With the maids a-stitching on the stair;
   The bread and biske', the beer and whiskey,
   Would make you frisky, if you were there;
   'Tis there you'd see Peg Murphy's daughter,
   A-washing pratees, fronent the door,
   With Roger Claery, and Father Healy,
   All blood relations to Lord Donoughmore.

6. There's statues gracing this noble place in,
   All heathen goddesses so fair,
   Bold Neptune, Plutarch, and Nicodemus,
   All standing naked in the open air;
   So now to finish this narration,
   Which my poor geni could not entwine,
   But were I a Homer, or Nebuchadnezzar,
   In ev'ry feature I would make it shine.

Although this favorite is known to most people in the setting by Flotow in his opera *Martha,* it is interesting to know that Mendelssohn also wrote a piano composition based on the same Irish tune. Mendelssohn composed his "Fantasy on an Irish Song," Op. 15, at the time of his first visit to the British Isles in 1829, about the same time that he made his first sketches of *The Hebrides,* his famous overture. These works and the *Scotch Symphony,* contrasting with his remarks during his trip, reveal Mendelssohn's ambivalence toward national music.

Anything but national music! Ten thousand devils take all such nationalism. Here I am in Wales, and oh how picturesque a harpist sits in the hallway of every tavern playing so-called folk melodies; that is to say, infamous, vulgar, rotten trash, while at the same time a hurdy-gurdy is also grinding out its melodies; enough to drive one mad; it has given me a toothache. The Scottish bagpipes, the Swiss cowhorns, the Welsh harps, all of them peddling their hunters' choruses and gruesome variations—the songs in the hall —all this eminently respectable music! It's unspeakable. Here I am, unable to bear Beethoven's national songs, and I come here and have to listen to the cawing of these screechy nasal instruments accompanied by ludicrous, asinine singers, and don't even swear!

The lyrics of the song were written by Mendelssohn's contemporary, Thomas Moore, in the collection of *Irish Melodies.* The poem was set to the tune known as "The Groves of Blarney." Beethoven also made a setting of the melody under the title "Sad and Luckless Was the Season" in the Thomson collection of Irish airs, and composed a set of variations on this tune, called erroneously *Air Ecossais,* no. 4 in *Six Varied Themes for Piano Alone, or with Flute or Violin,* op. 105.

III

SCOTTISH SONGS

Scottish folk song has two main language divisions, Gaelic of the Highlands and the tongue of the Lowland Scots. Whereas the music of the Highlanders has been preserved mainly through oral tradition, the songs from the Lowlands were early committed to paper. The latter were in an English dialect and therefore more accessible and popular in England, where the Scottish songs were first published in 1650. It was not until 1718, with the issuing of Allan Ramsay's *Tea-Table Miscellany* (Edinburgh, 1724–1727), that Scotland began printing its own song books. Several important collections followed. Among them were James Johnson's *Scots Musical Museum* (1787–1803) and George Thomson's *A Select Collection of Original Scottish Airs,* to both of which Robert Burns contributed over three hundred song texts and many tunes. Burns restored or amplified traditional lyrics and ballads, and wrote new ones to instrumental tunes. Sir Walter Scott and James Hogg, who was known as the Ettrick Shepherd, were among other poets who wrote for Thomson.

Hogg, like most of the Scottish poets, was a Jacobite—an ardent supporter of the House of Stuart in the struggle for the English and Scottish crown. He collected songs that were published in a book called *Jacobite Relics,* prefaced with the following description:

These songs are, moreover, a species of composition entirely by themselves. They have no affinity with our ancient ballads of heroism and romance; and one part of them far less with the mellow strains of our pastoral and lyric muses. Their general character is that of a rude, energetic humour that bids defiance to all opposition, in aims, sentiments, or rules of song-writing. They are the unmasked effusions of a bold and primitive race who hated and despised the overturning innovations that prevailed in Church and State, and held the abettors of these as dogs, or something worse . . . but there are among them specimens of sly and beautiful allegory. These last seem to have been sung openly and avowedly in mixed parties [in company of Loyalists—*ed.*] . . . while the others had been confined to the select social meeting of the confirmed Jacobites, or hoarded up in the cabinets of old Catholic families.

Among the other categories of Scottish song, the old ballads like "Barbara Allan" and "Lord Gregory" have ancient roots in common with England but have their own distinctive melodies and verbal expressions. The love songs, drinking songs, comic ditties and dance tunes are famous the world over for their beauty and earthy quality. A taste of the salty side of their character can be gleaned from the style of the comments of Hogg's mother to Sir Walter Scott:

There was never ane o' my sangs prentit till ye prentit them yoursel' and ye hae spoilt them awthegither. They were made for singin' an' no for readin'; but ye hae broken the charm noo, and they'll never [be] sung mair. An' the warst thing of a' they're nouther richt spell'd nor richt setten down.

The songs in this section may not be quite "richt" as they were once sung, but we are indeed fortunate that they were "setten down" by fine poets and composers.

15

JOCKEY AND JENNY

THOMAS D'URFEY (1653–1723)   HENRY PURCELL (1659–1695)

MUSIC AND TEXT SOURCE: *The Works of Henry Purcell*, Vol. XX, Novello & Co. Ltd., 1916.

JOCKEY AND JENNY

1. JOCKEY

A Jenny, gin you can love,
And have resolv'd you will try me,
Silly scruples remove
And do no longer deny me.

By thy bonny black eye,
I swear no other can move me;
Then, if you still deny,
You never, never did love me.

JENNY

B Jockey, how can you mistake,
That know full well when you woo me;
My poor head does so ache,
It throbs as it would come through me!

How can you be my friend,
That thus are bent to my ruin?
All the love you pretend
Is only for my undoing.

2. JOCKEY

A Who can tell by what art
This charming nothing called honour
Charms my Jenny's heart
When love and Jockey has won her?

JENNY

'Tis a toy in the head,
And muckle woe there's about it;
Yet I'd rather be dead
Than live in scandal without it.

B But if you'll love me and wed
And guard my honour from harms, too,
Jockey, I'll take to my bed,
And fold him close in my arms, too.

82

JOCKEY

Talk not of wedding, dear sweet;
No, I must have charms that are softer.
I'm not of a northerly breed,
And never shall love thee well after.

BOTH

B Then since ill fortune intends
Our amity shall be no dearer,
Still, let us kiss and be friends,
And sigh we shall never come nearer.

The dialogue of "Jockey and Jenny" in Act IV of the play *A Fool's Preferment* by D'Urfey (1688) is subtitled "A Scotch Song." The play is plagiarized with alterations from John Fletcher's *Noble Gentleman.*

Another version of the tune is found in John Johnson's *Collection of Two Hundred Dances* (1748), where its title is "Pot Stick."

There is also a musical setting of "Jocky and Jeany" in *Zwölfe schottische Volkslieder* by Max Bruch. In its present-day form it is known as "Come O'er The Stream, Charlie," one of the Jacobite songs collected by James Hogg.

16

PEGGY, I MUST LOVE THEE

(Weel My Willie Lo'es Me)

HENRY PURCELL (1659–1695)

MUSIC SOURCE: "A New Scotch Tune," from *Twelve Lessons for Harpsichord* (1687).

Vocal line and text added by the editor. Text from *Orpheus Caledonius* (1725).

life springs— up, he lifts his eyes With joy and waits —— her mo - tion.

1. As from a rock past all relief,
   The shipwrackt "Colin" spying
   His native soil, o'ercome with grief,
   Half sunk in waves, and dying:
   With the next morning sun he spies
   A ship which gives unhop'd surprise;
   New life springs up, he lifts his eyes
   With joy and waits her motion.

2. So when by her whom long I loved,
   I scorn'd was, and deserted,
   Low with despair my spirits mov'd,
   To be forever parted:
   Thus droopt I, till diviner grace
   I found in Peggy's mind and face;
   Ingratitude appear'd then base,
   But virtue more engaging.

3. Then now since happily I've hit,
   I'll have no more delaying;
   Let beauty yield to manly wit,
   We lose ourselves in staying.
   I'll haste dull courtship to a close,
   Since marriage can my fears oppose;
   Why should we happy minutes lose,
   Since, Peggy, I must love thee?

4. Men may be foolish if they please,
   And deem it a lover's duty
   To sigh and sacrifice their ease,
   Doting on a proud beauty:
   Such was my case for many a year,
   Still hope succeeding to my fear;
   False Betty's charms now disappear,
   Since Peggy's far outshines them.

1. Sing on, sing on, thou lark sae hie,   (. . . *so high*)
   Thy sang wi' love embues me,   (. . . *song* . . .)
   An' gars me aim to sing like thee   (. . . *causes me* . . .)
   How weel my Willie lo'es me.   (. . . *well my Willie loves me*)
   I wander by Tweed's siller tide,   (. . . *silver* . . .)
   My breast brim fu' o' gratefu' pride,
   For round me a' on ev'ry side
   Are proofs how Willie lo'es me.

2. He lo'ed me in his laddie days,
      An' still he fondly woos me;
   Tweed's winding vales an' flow'ry braes   (*slope of a hill*)
      Can tell how weel he lo'es me.
   He decks my brow wi' jewels rare;
   He tends me wi' a lover's care;
   My heart is his for evermair—   (. . . *for evermore*)
      For weel I know he lo'es me.

3. Frae day to day, frae year to year,   (. . . *from* . . .)
      His kindness still endues me
   Wi' some new gift that tells how dear
      I am to him wha lo'es me.   (. . . *who loves me*)
   An' yon fair ha' he's biggit me,   (. . . *hall he's built for me*)
   That tow'rs o'er a' sae proud an' hie,
   Will let a' future ages see
      How weel my Willie lo'es me.

from: *One Hundred Songs* by James Ballantine (John S. Marr, Glasgow, 1866)

The tune and harmonization is in *Musick's Handmaid,* Part II (1687) from Purcell's *Twelve Lessons for the Harpsichord* of which this one is titled "A New Scotch Tune." The melody and text of "Peggy," was printed in *Orpheus Caledonius* in 1725. The text of "Tom and Will" is found with the same tune in D'Urfey's *Wit and Mirth* (1719-1720). Stenhouse claims that it was written by Henry Playford, who adapted it to the Scottish air. To the words "How cruel is that parent's care" it was sung in the William Bates' play *The Jovial Crew* (1731).

What starts out as a simple pentatonic melody gives us some surprises in the last five measures with its ambivalence between minor and major, and the lowered and raised 7th degree of the scale.

17

'TWAS WITHIN A FURLONG OF EDINBOROUGH TOWN

THOMAS D'URFEY (1653–1723)

HENRY PURCELL (1659–1695)

1. 'Twas with - in a fur - long of E - din - bo - rough Town In the ros - ie time of year when the grass __ was __ down, Bon - ny Jock - y blithe and gay Said to Jen - ny mak - ing hay, "Let's __

MUSIC AND TEXT SOURCE: *Deliciae Musicae*, 1696.

sit a lit - tle, dear, and prat - tle, 'tis a sul - try day!" He ____

long had court - ed the black - brow'd ____ maid, But

Jock - y was a wag and would ne'er con - sent to wed; Which ____

made her pish and phoo, And cry out "It will not do, I ____

can - not,　can - not,　can - not,　won - not,　mon - not　buck - le　to.''

1. 'Twas within a furlong of Edinborough Town
   In the rosie time of year when the grass was down,
   Bonny Jocky blithe and gay
   Said to Jenny making hay,
   "Let's sit a little, dear, and prattle, 'tis a sultry day."
   He long had courted the black-brow'd maid,
   But Jocky was a wag and would ne'er consent to wed;
   Which made her pish and phoo,
   And cry out, "It will not do,
   I cannot, cannot, cannot, wonnot, monnot buckle to."

       (. . . *will   not,*
       must not give in)

2. He told her marriage was grown a mere joke,
   And that no one wedded now, but the scoundrel folk;
   "Yet, my dear, thou should'st prevail,
   But I know not what I ail,
   I shall dream of clogs and silly dogs with bottles at their tail;
   But I'll give thee gloves and a bongrace to wear,
   And a pretty filly foal to ride out and take the air,
   If thou ne'er will pish and phoo
   And cry, 'It ne'er shall do,
   I cannot, cannot, cannot, wonnot, monnot buckle to'."

3. "That you'll give me trinkets," cried she, "I believe.
   But ah! what in return must your poor Jenny give?
   When my maiden treasure's gone,
   I must gang to London Town,
   And roar and rant, and patch and paint, and kiss for half a crown;
   Each drunken bully oblige for pay,
   And earn a hated living in an odious fulsom way.
   No, no, no, it ne'er shall do,
   For a wife I'll be to you,
   Or I cannot, cannot, cannot, wonnot, monnot buckle to."

The play *The Mock Marriage* by Thomas Scott, which was presented in 1696, included the song in the setting by Purcell. In the same year, titled "A Scotch Tune," the music with text was printed in Playford's *Deliciae Musicae* (Vol. III) and a few years later in D'Urfey's *Wit and Mirth*. Subsequently, James Hook wrote another melody with a variant of the text, which became popular and supplanted the original tune in many publications.

A moralizing posture was then, as now, the guise for many a bawdy song. The Restoration period saw much license, a reaction to the repression of the Cromwell regime.

18

BARB'RA ALLAN

JOSEF HAYDN (1732–1809)

1. 'Twas in and a - bout the __ Mar - t'mas __ time, When the green leaves were __ a - fall - ing, That Sir John Graeme in the West __ coun - try, Fell in love with Bar - b'ra __ Al - lan. He

MUSIC AND TEXT SOURCE: G. Thomson; and Wm. Napier, *Selection of Original Scots Songs* (1790); also, *Joseph Haydn Werke,* Series XXXII, Vol. I, No. 11, G. Henle.

sent his man down thro' the town, To the place where she was

dwell - ing — "O haste, and come to my

mas - ter dear, __ Gin __ ye be Bar - b'ra Al - lan."

Vln.

D. S. (or segue)

1. 'Twas in and about the Mart'mas time,
   When the green leaves were a-falling,
   That Sir John Graeme, in the west country,
   Fell in love with Barb'ra Allan.
   He sent his man down thro' the town,
   To the place where she was dwelling—
   "O haste and come to my master dear,
   Gin ye be Barb'ra Allan."   *(If . . .)*

2. O hooly, hooly gaed she up,   *(. . . slowly, slowly she went up)*
   To the place where he was lying,
   And when she drew the curtain by,—
   "Young man, I think you're dying!"
   "O it's I'm sick, and very, very sick,
   And 'tis a' for Barb'ra Allan!"
   "O the better for me ye's never be
   Tho' your heart's blood were a-spilling!"

3. "O dinna ye mind, young man," said she,   *(. . . don't you remember . . .)*
   "When ye in the tavern was drinking,
   That ye made the healths gae round and round,
   And slighted Barb'ra Allan!"
   He turn'd his face unto the wall,
   And death was with him dealing:—
   "Adieu, adieu, my dear friends all,
   And be kind to Barb'ra Allan!"

4. And slowly, slowly raise she up,
   And slowly, slowly left him,
   And sighing, said, she could not stay,
   Since death of life had reft him.
   She had not gaen a mile but twa,   *(. . . gone a mile or two)*
   When she heard the dead-bell ringing,
   And ev'ry jow that the dead-bell gied,   *(. . . peal the death-bell gave)*
   It cried, "Woe to Barb'ra Allan!"

5. "O mother, mother, make my bed,
   O make it saft and narrow;   *(. . . soft . . .)*
   Since my love died for me today,
   I'll die for him tomorrow!"

This is one of the oldest and most popular ballads still current among English singing people. Through wide dissemination, it has given birth to numerous offspring.
Francis James Child in his classic work *English and Scottish Popular Ballads*
(1882–1898) includes two familiar versions. Cecil Sharp alone had collected as
many as twenty-seven. Bertrand Bronson in his encyclopedic work, *The Traditional*

Tunes of the Child Ballads (Princeton, 1959), presents 198 variants, among them pieces with such titles as "Bonny Barbara Allan," "The Cruelty of Barbara Allen," "Barbarous Ellen," etc.

An entry in Pepys' diary for January 2, 1666 reads: "In perfect pleasure I was to hear her sing, and especially her little Scotch song of Barbary Allen." About a century later, Goldsmith writes: "The music of the finest singer is dissonance to what I felt when our old dairy-maid sung me unto tears with . . . 'The Cruelty of Barbara Allen.' "

The earliest printed text is in Allen Ramsay's *The Tea-Table Miscellany* (1724– 1740). The music first appears in print in *The Caledonian Pocket Companion,* Book II (1750) of James Oswald.

Haydn made two settings of the ballad, the first in William Napier's *Selection of Original Scots Songs* (1790–1792). In that book, as in most editions, the text is in quatrains. However, in the later publication by George Thomson of *A Select Collection of Original Scottish Airs* (1799–1805), Haydn's arrangement is set to eight-line stanzas, leaving us with the puzzle of how to handle the last verse of only four lines. Thomson would often "refine" the text as well as the music, inviting poets to compose new lyrics. Gilbert Elliot was selected to "improve" upon the traditional poem, and his efforts are introduced with the following notice: "These pathetic verses appear to the editor better suited to this fine air." The two Haydn settings are placed side by side in our collection. The one from the Napier book has been transposed from D minor to C minor to permit it to be performed in sequence with the other setting. The two arrangements offer interesting contrast in treatment, the accompaniment in one being chordal while the second is contrapuntal with more movement. Alternating them for successive verses would vary and enhance the performance, and by ending with the second (Napier) version the problem of the dangling four lines of the last verse can be solved.

19

GREEN GROW THE RASHES, O

ROBERT BURNS (1759–1796)

JOSEF HAYDN (1732–1809)

Allegretto piuttosto vivace

1. There's nought but care on ev-'ry han', In ev-'ry hour that pass-es, O; What
2. The warl'-ly race may rich-es chase, An' rich-es still may fly them, O; An'

sig - ni - fies the life o' man, An 'twere na for the lass-es, O?
tho' at last they catch them fast, Their hearts can ne'er en - joy them, O.

(CHORUS)

Green grow the rash - es, O! Green __ grow the rash - es, O! The

MUSIC AND TEXT SOURCE: G. Thomson; also *Joseph Haydn Werke*, Series XXXII, Vol. I, No. 11,
G. Henle.

sweet - est hours that e'er I spend, Are spent a - mang the lass - es, O!

CHORUS

Green grow the rash - es, O! Green___ grow the rash - es, O! The

sweet - est hours that e'er I spend, Are spent a - mang the lass - es, O!

D. S.

1. There's nought but care on ev'ry han',
   In ev'ry hour that passes, O;
   What signifies the life o' man,
   An 'twere na for the lasses, O? *(if it were not . . .)*

CHORUS: Green grow the rashes, O! *(. . . rushes . . .)*
         Green grow the rashes, O!
         The sweetest hours that e'er I spend,
         Are spent amang the lasses, O! *Chorus:*

2. The warl'y race may riches chase, *(. . . worldly . . .)*
   An' riches still may fly them, O;
   An' tho' at last they catch them fast,
   Their hearts can ne'er enjoy them, O. *Chorus:*

3. But gie me a cannie hour at e'en, *(. . . give me a quiet . . .)*
   My arms about my dearie, O;
   An' warl'y cares, an' warl'y men,
   May a' gae tapsateerie, O! *Chorus:* *(. . . topsy-turvy . . .)*

4. For you sae douce, ye sneer at this, *(. . . sober . . .)*
   Ye're nought but senseless asses, O;
   The wisest man the warl' saw,
   He dearly lov'd the lasses, O! *Chorus:*

5. Auld Nature swears, the lovely dears
   Her noblest work she classes, O:
   Her prentice han' she tried on man,
   An' then she made the lasses, O. *Chorus:*

George Thomson, assuming editorial prerogative in his collection of *Scottish Airs,* omitted the final "O" in the alternate lines of the verses and three lines of the chorus of the Burns poem. As a result, the final note in the corresponding phrases of the tune is lacking. These have been restored, inserted in small notes, by the present editor. They were not in the Haydn arrangement that was written to Thomson's version; but the syllable and note are found in the chorus of an earlier Haydn setting for the Napier collection:

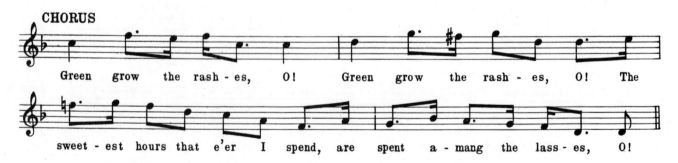

Burns based his verses on the following early rustic song, a satire on the profligacy of the priests prior to the Reformation.

We're a' dry wi' drinkin' o't,   Green grow the rashes, O,
We're a' dry wi' drinkin' o't,   Green grow the rashes, O,
The parson kissed the fiddler's wife   A feather bed is nae sae saft
And could na preach for thinkin' o't.   As a bed amang the rashes, O.

20

MAGGIE LAUDER

JOSEF HAYDN (1732–1809)

Allegretto spiritoso

1. Wha wad - na be in love Wi' bon - nie Mag - gie Lau - der? A pip - er met her gaun to Fife, And spier'd what was't they ca'd her. Right scorn - ful - ly she an - swer'd him,— "Be-

MUSIC AND TEXT SOURCE: G. Thomson; also *Joseph Haydn Werke,* Series XXXII, Vol. I, No. 11, G. Henle.

gone, ye hal - lan - sha - ker! Jog__ on your gate, ye blad - der-skate, My

name is Mag - gie Lau - der."

1. Wha wadna be in love   *(Who would not . . .)*
   Wi' bonnie Maggie Lauder?
   A piper met her gaun to Fife,   *(. . . goin' . . .)*
   And spier'd what was't they ca'd her.   *(. . . asked . . . called)*
   Right scornfully she answer'd him,—
   "Begone, ye hallanshaker!   *(. . . vagrant, bum . . .)*
   Jog on your gate, ye bladderskate,   *(on your way, you foolish talker)*
   My name is Maggie Lauder."

2. "Maggie," quo' he, "and by my bags,
   I'm fidging fain to see thee!   *(. . . restless to see you)*
   Sit down by me, my bonnie bird,
   In troth I winna steer thee: *(. . . I will not stir you)*
   For I'm a piper to my trade,
   My name is Rob the Ranter;
   The lasses loup as they were daft   *(. . . leap as if crazy)*
   When I blow up my chanter."

3. "Piper," quo' Meg, "hae ye your bags,
   Or is your drone in order?
   If you be Rob, I've heard of you,—
   Live you upo' the Border?
   The lasses a' baith far and near   *(. . . all both . . .)*
   Have heard of Rob the Ranter;
   I'll shake my foot wi' right good will,
   Gin you'll blaw up your chanter."   *(If you'll blow . . .)*

4. Then to his bags he flew wi' speed,   *(. . . bagpipes . . .)*
   About the drone he twisted;
   Meg up, and wallop'd o'er the green,   *(. . . moved quickly . . .)*
   For brawly could she frisk it.   *(. . . smartly . . . jump)*
   "Weel done," quo' he—"Play up," quo' she:
   "Weel bobb'd," quo' Rob the Ranter: *(Well danced . . .)*
   "It's worth my while to play indeed,
   When I hae sic a dancer."   *(When I have such . . .)*

5. "Weel hae ye play'd your part," quo' Meg,   *(Well have . . .)*
   "Your cheeks are like the crimson;
   There's nane in Scotland plays so weel,   *(. . . none . . .)*
   Since we lost Habby Simson.
   I've lived in Fife, baith maid and wife,   *(. . . both . . .)*
   These ten years and a quarter,
   Gin ye should come to Anster fair,   *(If . . .)*
   Spier ye for Maggy Lauder."   *(Ask . . .)*

The first printing of the song's text was by David Herd in Edinburgh (1769). The poem is often credited to Francis Semple as having been written in 1642. But there is no evidence of this, other than the belief of his grandchildren, whose testimony has proved questionable because of their other unfounded claims of authorship.

There are several references in the song to the bagpipes and to its various parts. The main sections of the bagpipes are: the blow-pipe (or sometimes a bellows) for producing the wind; the bag for storing the wind; the two or more drones, each of which sustains a single tone; and the chanter, which is a pipe with a double reed and fingerholes for playing the melody. The bagpipes, like the fiddle in folk poetry, here has double meanings with erotic symbolism.

21

OH, HAD I A CAVE

(Robin Adair) *(While Larks with Little Wings)*
(Erin, the Tear and the Smile in Thine Eyes)

ROBERT BURNS (1759–1796)

JOSEF HAYDN (1732–1809)

1. Oh had I a cave on some wild dis- tant shore, Where the winds howl to the wave's dash-ing roar;
2. Fals- est of wo- man-kind, can'st thou de- clare All thy fond plight- ed vows fleet- ing as air!

MUSIC AND TEXT SOURCE: G. Thomson; also *Joseph Haydn Werke*, Series XXXII, Vol. I, No. 11, G. Henle.

There would I weep my woes, There seek my ___
To thy new lov - er hie, Laugh o'er thy ___

lost re - pose, Till grief ___ my ___ eyes should close,
per - ju - ry ___ Then in ___ thy ___ bos - om try

Ne'er to wake more.
What peace is there.

Oh, Had - 2

1. Had I a cave on some wild distant shore,
    Where the winds howl to the wave's dashing roar;
        There would I weep my woes,
        There seek my lost repose,
        Till grief my eyes should close,
            Ne'er to wake more.

2. Falsest of womankind, cans't thou declare
    All thy fond plighted vows fleeting as air!
        To thy new lover hie,
        Laugh o'er thy perjury—
        Then in thy bosom try
            What peace is there.

ROBIN ADAIR

ROBERT BURNS

1. What's this dull town to me?
    Robin's not near.
    What was't I wished to see?
    What wished to hear?
    Where all the joy and mirth
    Made this town heav'n on earth?
    Oh, they're all fled wi' thee,
    Robin Adair.

2. What made th'assembly shine?
    Robin Adair.
    What made the ball so fine?
    Robin was there.
    What when the play was o'er,
    What made my heart so sore?
    Oh, it was parting with
    Robin Adair.

3. But now thou'rt cold to me,
    Robin Adair,
    But now thou'rt cold to me,
    Robin Adair.
    Yet he I loved so well
    Still in my heart shall dwell;
    Oh, I can ne'er forget
    Robin Adair.

WHILE LARKS WITH LITTLE WINGS

ROBERT BURNS

1. While larks with little wings
   Fann'd the pure air,
   Viewing the breathing spring,
   Forth I did fare:
   Gay, the sun's golden eye
   Peep'd o'er the mountains high;
   "Such thy bloom," did I cry—
   "Phillis the fair."

2. In each bird's careless song,
   Glad did I share;
   While yon wild-flowers among,
   Chance led me there:
   Sweet to the opening day,
   Rosebuds bent the dewy spray;
   "Such thy bloom," did I say—
   "Phillis the fair."

3. Down in a shady walk
   Doves cooing were;
   I mark'd the cruel hawk
   Caught in a snare:
   So kind may Fortune be,
   Such make his destiny,
   He who would injure thee,
   Phillis the fair.

ERIN, THE TEAR AND THE SMILE IN THINE EYES

THOMAS MOORE

1. Erin, the tear and the smile in thine eyes
   Blend like the rainbow that hangs in the skies;
   Shining through sorrow's stream,
   Sadd'ning through pleasure's beam,
   Thy suns, with doubtful gleam,
   Weep while they rise!

2. Erin! thy silent tear never shall cease,
   Erin! thy languid smile ne'er shall increase,
   Till, like the rainbow's light,
   Thy various tints unite,
   And form in Heaven's sight
   One arch of peace!

Oh, Had I a Cave

The tune is known both as the Scottish "Robin Adair" and the Irish "Aileen aroon." The melody under the latter title is first found in the *Caledonian Pocket Companion,* 1753. The poem was written by Burns for *Scottish Airs,* 1799.

Robin Adair

In the course of time, the cadences of the song have acquired ornamental notes with the "Scotch snap," as it is familiar today in the following example at*:

While Larks with Little Wings

Burns, in a note to Thomson in 1793 on the origins of the tune, wrote: "I have met with a musical Highlander in Breadalbane's Fencibles, which are quartered here, who assures me that he well remembers his mother singing Gaelic songs to both Robin Adair and Gramachree. They certainly have more of the Scots than the Irish taste in them. . . . What I shrewdly suspect to be the case—the wandering minstrels, harpers, or pipers, used to go frequently errant through the wilds both of Scotland and Ireland and so some favourite airs might be common to both."

Erin, the Tear and the Smile in Thine Eyes

Thomas Moore paraphrased the traditional Irish songs in much the same way as Burns did the Scottish. Both had a passion for national identity and freedom which inspired their lyrics. This song is based on "Aileen aroon," in which the Celtic phrase "Ceud mile failte, Eilean mo run" means "a hundred thousand welcomes, island of my love."

22

UP IN THE MORNING EARLY

(The Scotchman Outwitted)

ROBERT BURNS (1759–1796)   JOSEF HAYDN (1732–1809)

1. Cauld blaws the wind frae east to west, The drift is driv-ing sair - ly, Sae loud and shrill's I hear the blast I'm

2. The birds sit chit - t'ring in the thorn, A' day they fare but spare - ly; And lang's the night frae e'en to morn I'm

MUSIC AND TEXT SOURCE: Wm. Napier, *Selection of Original Scots Songs* (1790–1792); also *Joseph Haydn Werke*, Series XXXII, Vol. 1, No. 28, G. Henle.

sure _____ it's win - ter fair - ly.
sure _____ it's win - ter fair - ly!

CHORUS

Up in the morn - ing's no _____ for me,

Up in the morn - ing ear - ly! When a' _____ the hills are

cov - er'd wi' snaw, I'm _____ sure it's _____ win - ter fair - ly!

[l.h.]

1. Cauld blaws the wind frae east to west,   (*Cold blows the wind from* . . .)
   The drift is driving sairly,   (. . . *severely*)
   Sae loud and shrill's I hear the blast—
   I'm sure it's winter fairly.

CHORUS   Up in the morning's no for me,   (. . . *not for me*)
         Up in the morning early!
         When a' the hills are cover'd wi' snaw,   (. . . *with snow*)
         I'm sure it's winter fairly!

2. The birds sit chitt'ring in the thorn,   (. . . *shivering* . . .)
   A' day they fare but sparely;
   And lang's the night frae e'en to morn—   (. . . *long's the night from evening* . . .)
   I'm sure it's winter fairly!

THE SCOTCHMAN OUTWITTED BY THE FARMER'S DAUGHTER

1. Cold and raw the North did blow,
   Bleak in the morning early,
   All the hills were hid with snow,
   Cover'd with winter yearly;
   As I was riding o'er the slough,
   I met with a farmer's daughter,
   Rosy cheeks, and a bonny brow,
   Good faith, my mouth did water.

2. Down I vail'd my bonnet low,
   Meaning to show my breeding;
   She return'd a graceful bow,
   Her visage far exceeding:
   I ask'd her where she was going so soon,
   And long'd to hold a parley;
   She told me, to the next market-town,
   On purpose to sell her barley.

3. "In this purse, sweet soul," said I,
   "Twenty pounds lie fairly;
   Seek no further one to buy,
   For Ise take all thy barley: (. . . *I shall* . . .)
   Twenty pound more shall purchase delight,
   Thy person I love so dearly,
   If thou wilt lie with me all night,
   And gang home in the morning early."   (*And go* . . .)

4. "If forty pound would buy the globe,
   This thing I would not do, sir;
   Or were my friends as poor as Job,
   I'd never raise 'em so, sir;
   For should you prove one night my friend,
   Wese get a young kid together;   (*We would get* . . .)
   And you'd be gone ere nine months end,
   Then where should I find the father?

5. "Pray, what would my parents say,
   If I should be so silly
   To give my maidenhead away,
   And lose my true-love Billy?
   Oh, this would bring me to disgrace,
   And therefore I say you nay, sir:
   And if that you would me embrace,
   First marry, and then you may, sir."

6. I told her, I had wedded been
   Fourteen years, and longer;
   Else I'd choose her for my queen,
   And tie the knot more stronger.
   She bid me then no farther come,
   But manage my wedlock fairly,
   And keep my purse for poor spouse at home,
   For some other should buy her barley.

7. Then, as swift as any roe,
   She rode away and left me;
   After her I could not go,
   Of joy she quite bereft me:
   Thus I myself did disappoint,
   For she did leave me fairly;
   My words knock'd all things out of joint,
   I lost both maid and barley.

8. Riding down a narrow lane,
   Some two or three hours after,
   There I chanc'd to meet again
   This farmer's bonny daughter:
   Although it was both raw and cold,
   I stay'd to hold a parley,
   And show'd once more my purse of gold,
   When as she had sold her barley.

9. "Love," said I "pray do not frown,
   But let us change embraces;
   I'll buy thee a fine silken gown,
   With ribbons, gloves, and laces,
   A ring and bodkin, muff and fan,
   No lady shall have neater;
   For, as I am an honest man,
   I ne'er saw a sweeter creature."

10. Then I took her by the hand,
    And said, "My dearest jewel,
    Why should'st thou thus disputing stand?
    I prithee be not cruel."
    She found my mind was wholly bent

To pleasure my fond desire,
Therefore she seemed to consent,
But I wish I had never come nigh her.

11. "Sir," she said, "what shall I do,
If I commit this evil,
And yield myself in love with you?
I hope you will prove civil.
You talk of ribbons, gloves, and rings,
And likewise gold and treasure;
Oh, let me first enjoy those things,
And then you shall have pleasure."

12. "Sure thy will shall be obey'd,"
Said I, "my own dear honey,"
Then into her lap I laid
Full forty pounds in money;
"We'll to the market-town this day,
And straightway end this quarrel,
And deck thee like a lady gay,
In flourishing rich apparel."

13. All my gold and silver there
To her I did deliver;
On the road we did repair,
Out-coming to a river,
Whose waters are both deep and wide,
Such rivers I ne'er see many;
She leaped her mare on the other side,
And left me not one penny.

14. Then my heart was sunk full low,
With grief and care surrounded;
After her I could not go
For fear of being drowned.
She turn'd about and said, "Behold,
I am not for your devotion;
But, sir, I thank you for your gold,
'Twill serve to enlarge my portion."

15. I began to stamp and stare,
To see what she had acted;
With my hands I tore my hair,
Like one that was distracted:
"Give me my money," then I cried,
"Good faith I did but lend it."
But she full fast away did ride,
And vow'd she did not intend it.

from: *A Select Collection of English Songs* by Joseph Ritson, London, 1813

Haydn's setting appears in Napier's *A Selection of Original Scots Songs*, Vol. II. Although the earliest printed source of the song was in the English collection *Dancing Master* (1651) with the title of "Stingo, or the Oyle of Barley," J. C. Dick in his authoritative book on Burns argues that, according to circumstantial evidence, it is probably of Scottish origin. As early as 1688, it was called a Scotch tune in an English publication. The music was not printed in Scotland before 1755 and the text not before Burns's time. This points up the fact that the provenance of a folk song is not necessarily indicated by its first printing.

Dr. Charles Burney, in his *General History of Music* (1789), recounts the following:

It is said that Queen Mary having expressed herself warmly in favour of the old Scots tune of "Cold and raw the wind doth blow" [as it was then known], Purcell made it a perpetual base [*sic*] to an air in the next birthday ode, 1692, beginning "May her blest example chase:" a piece of pleasantry which is likewise said to have been occasioned by her majesty's asking for this tune after Mr. Gostling, one of the gentlemen of the Chapel Royal, and the celebrated Mrs. Arabella Hunt, with Purcell to accompany them on the harpsichord, had exerted all their talents and abilities to amuse so great a personage with compositions they mistakenly thought of a superior class.

Stenhouse assumes that Purcell got the idea of using this tune as a bass from John Hilton's "Northern Catch" for three voices, "I'se gae with thee, my sweet Peggy," in which "Up in the Morning" is in the third voice.

ODE FOR QUEEN MARY'S BIRTHDAY (1692)　　　　　　　　　　　H. Purcell

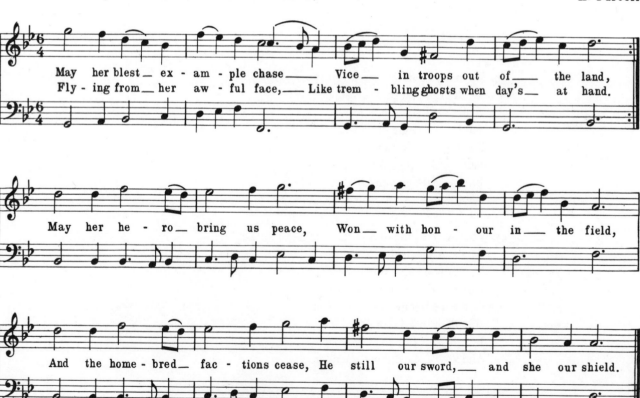

23

BONNY LADDIE, HIGHLAND LADDIE

(Geordie Sits in Charlie's Chair)

JAMES HOGG (1770–1835)   LUDWIG VAN BEETHOVEN (1770–1827)

1. Where got ye that sil - ver moon, Bon - ny lad - die,____
2. Weels - me - on yon tar - tan trews, Bon - ny lad - die,____

High - land lad - die! Glint - ing braw your belt __ a __ boon,
High - land lad - die! Tell me, tell me a'__ the __ news,

MUSIC AND TEXT SOURCE: G. Thomson, also *Beethoven's Werke*, Breitkopf and Härtel.

1. Where got ye that silver moon,
   Bonny laddie, Highland laddie!
   Glinting braw your belt a boon,   *(Handsome above your belt . . .)*
   Bonny laddie, Highland laddie!
   Belted plaid and bonnet blue,
   Bonny laddie, Highland laddie!
   Have ye been at Waterloo?
   Bonny laddie, Highland laddie!

2. Weels-me-on yon tartan trews,   *(. . . trousers)*
   Bonny laddie, Highland laddie!
   Tell me, tell me a' the news,
   Bonny laddie, Highland laddie!
   Saw ye Bony by the way!
   Bonny laddie, Highland laddie!
   Blucher wi' his beard so grey?
   Bonny laddie, Highland laddie!

3. Or that dour and deadly duke,
   Bonny laddie, Highland laddie!
   Scatt'ring Frenchmen wi' his look,
   Bonny laddie, Highland laddie!
   Some, says he, the day may rue,
   Bonny laddie, Highland laddie!
   Who can tell gin this be true?
   Bonny laddie, Highland laddie!

4. Would ye tell me, gin ye ken,   *(. . . if you know)*
   Bonny laddie, Highland laddie!
   Aught o' Donald and his men,
   Bonny laddie, Highland laddie!
   Tell me o' my kilted clan,
   Bonny laddie, Highland laddie!
   Gin they fought or gin they ran?
   Bonny laddie, Highland laddie!

HIGHLAND LADDIE (Loyalist Song)

1. When you came over first frae France,   *(. . . from . . .)*
      Bonny laddie, Highland laddie!
   You swore to lead our King a dance,
      Bonny laddie, Highland laddie,
   And promis'd on your royal word,
      Bonny laddie, Highland laddie,
   To make the Duke dance o'er the sword,
      Bonny laddie, Highland laddie.

117

2. When he to you began to play,
     Bonny laddie, Highland laddie,
You quat the green and ran away,   (. . . *quit* . . .)
     Bonny laddie, Highland laddie;
The dance thus turn'd into a chace,
     Bonny laddie, Highland laddie,
It must be own'd you wan the race,
     Bonny laddie, Highland laddie.

3. Your partners that came o'er frae France,
     Bonny laddie, Highland laddie,
They understood not a Scots dance,
     Bonny laddie, Highland laddie;
Therefore their complaisance to shew
     Bonny laddie, Highland laddie,
Unto the Duke they bow'd right low,
     Bonny laddie, Highland laddie.

4. If e'er you come to dance again,
     Bonny laddie, Highland laddie,
New dancers you must bring frae Spain,
     Bonny laddie, Highland laddie,
And, that all things may be secure,
     Bonny laddie, Highland laddie,
See that your dancers be not poor,
     Bonny laddie, Highland laddie.

5. I think insurance you can make,
     Bonny laddie, Highland laddie,
Lest dancing you should break your neck,
     Bonny laddie, Highland laddie,
For he that dances on a rope,
     Bonny laddie, Highland laddie;
Should not trust all unto the Pope,
     Bonny laddie, Highland laddie.

6. For dancing you were never made,
     Bonny laddie, Highland laddie,
Then, while 'tis time, leave off the trade,
     Bonny laddie, Highland laddie;
Be thankful for your last escape,
     Bonny laddie, Highland laddie,
And like your * brother take a cape.

from: William Stenhouse, notes in
Scots Musical Museum

* Cardinal York

GEORDIE SITS IN CHARLIE'S CHAIR (Jacobite Song)

1. Geordie sits in Charlie's chair
       Bonny laddie, Highland laddie,
   Deil cock him gin he sit there,   *(Devil take him if. . . .)*
       Bonny laddie, Highland laddie;
   Charlie yet shall mount the throne,
       Bonny laddie, Highland laddie,
   Weel ye ken it is his own,   *(Well you know . . .)*
       Bonny laddie, Highland laddie.

2. Weary fa' the Lawland loon,   *(Weary falls the Lowland rascal)*
       Bonny laddie, Highland laddie,
   Whae took frae him the British crown,   *(Who took from him . . .)*
       Bonny laddie, Highland laddie;
   But weels me on the kilted clans,   *(But I wish well . . .)*
       Bonny laddie, Highland laddie,
   That fought for him at Prestonplans,
       Bonny laddie, Highland laddie.

3. Ken ye the news I hae to tell?   *(Know you . . . have . . .)*
       Bonny laddie, Highland laddie,
   Cumberland's awa to hell,   *(. . . away . . .)*
       Bonny laddie, Highland laddie.
   When he came to Stygian shore,
       Bonny laddie, Highland laddie,
   The deil himsel' wi' fright did roar,
       Bonny laddie, Highland laddie.

4. Then Charon grim came out to him,
       Bonny laddie, Highland laddie,
   "Ye're welcome here, ye deil's limb!"
       Bonny laddie, Highland laddie;
   They put on him a philabeg,   *(. . . kilt)*
       Bonny laddie, Highland laddie,
   And in his doup they ca'd a peg,   *(And in his bottom they drove . . .)*
       Bonny laddie, Highland laddie.

5. How he did skip and he did roar!
       Bonny laddie, Highland laddie,
   The deils ne'er saw sic sport before,   *(. . . such sport . . .)*
       Bonny laddie, Highland laddie;
   They took him neist to Satan's ha'   *(. . . next to Satan's hall)*
       Bonny laddie, Highland laddie,
   To lilt it wi' his grandpapa,   *(To sing along with . . .)*
       Bonny laddie, Highland laddie.

6. The deil sat grinning in his neuk,   (. . . *nook*)
        Bonny laddie, Highland laddie,
   Riving sticks to roast the Duke,
        Bonny laddie, Highland laddie;
   They pat him neist upon a spit,   (. . . *put him next* . . .)
        Bonny laddie, Highland laddie,
   And roasted him baith head and feet,   (. . . *both* . . .)
        Bonny laddie, Highland laddie.

7. Wi' scalded brunstane and wi' fat,   (. . . *brimstone* . . .)
        Bonny laddie, Highland laddie,
   They flamm'd his carcass weel wi' that;
        Bonny laddie, Highland laddie;
   They ate him up baith stoop and roop,   (. . . *both dish and ?*)
        Bonny laddie, Highland laddie,
   And that's the gate they serv'd the Duke,   (*And that's the way* . . .)
        Bonny laddie, Highland laddie.

James Hogg (1770–1835), who wrote the poem for "Bonny Laddie, Highland Laddie" and several other of Beethoven's arrangements of Scottish songs, was known as the Ettrick Shepherd. In his book *Jacobite Relics,* he cites the following verse as the oldest version of the song:

> I canna get my mare ta'en,
>   Bonnie laddie, Highland laddie,
> Master had she never nane,
>   Bonnie laddie, Highland laddie.

A note by Burns says:

It is singular enough that the Scottish muses were all Jacobites. I have paid more attention to every description of Scots songs than perhaps anybody living has done, and I do not recollect one single stanza, nor even the title of the most trifling Scots air, which has the least panegyrical reference to the families of Nassau or Brunswick; while there are hundreds satirizing them. This may be thought no panegyric on the Scots poets; but I mean it as such.

William Stenhouse, despite his admiration for Burns, contradicts him by offering evidence of three Scottish Loyalist songs. The text of one of them is given above, starting with the lines:

> When you came over first frae France,
>   Bonny laddie, Highland laddie,

At any rate, the preponderance of Scottish songs were Jacobite.

In the *Jacobite Songs* by Charles Mackay (1861) there is a dialogue song under the title "Lowland Lassie," the first verse of which runs:

> The cannons roar and trumpets sound,
> Bonnie lassie, Lowland lassie,
> And a' the hills wi' Charles resound,
> Bonnie lassie, Lowland lassie, etc.

Geordie, as he is named in several Jacobite songs, refers to George II of the house of Hanover. His opponent was Charlie, or Prince Charles of the house of Stuart.

The song in Thomson's *Scottish Airs* seems to be a later version by Hogg, the text referring to the Napoleonic War, "Bony" of course being Bonaparte, and Blucher the marshal who aided Wellington at Waterloo.

The final E of the melody in Beethoven's setting is out of keeping with the rest of the hexatonic tune. In most collections the tune ends on C. Beethoven also composed a set of variations based on this tune, *Air Ecossais*, no. 2 in *Ten Varied Themes for Piano Alone, or with Flute or Violin,* op. 107.

There are two humorous verses from Blackie's *Book of Scottish Songs* that are worth presenting:

> To ha'e a wife and rule a wife,
> Taks a wise man, taks a wise man,
> But to get a wife to rule a man,
> O that ye can, O that ye can.
> So the wifes that's wise we aye maun prize,   (. . . *must* . . .)
> For they're few ye ken, they're scarce ye ken:
> O Solomon says ye'll no fin' ane   (. . . *find one*)
> In hundreds ten, in hundreds ten.

> Sae he that gets a guid, guid wife,
> Gets gear eneugh, gets gear eneugh;
> An' he that gets an ill, ill wife,
> Gets cares eneugh, get fears eneugh.
> A man may spen', an' ha'e to the en',
> If his wife be ought, if his wife be ought;
> But a man may spare, an' aye be bare
> If his wife be nought, if his wife be nought.

Besides serving partisan politics and homespun philosophy, this popular tune also helped the shantyman pass the long hours on the boats between England and Canada as he sang:

> Were you ever to Quebec,
> Donkey riding, donkey riding,
> Storing timber on the deck,
> Riding on a donkey?

24

COME FILL, FILL, MY GOOD FELLOW

(Three Gude Fellows)

(The Town Drummer)

WILLIAM SMYTH (C. 1800)   LUDWIG VAN BEETHOVEN (1770–1827)

Spiritoso, ma non troppo presto

Come fill, fill, my good fel-low! Fill high, high, my good fel-low! And

let's be mer-ry and mel-low, And let us have one bot-tle more. When

warm the heart is flow-ing, And bright the fan-cy glow-ing, Oh!

MUSIC AND TEXT SOURCE: G. Thomson, also *Beethoven's Werke*, Breitkopf and Härtel.

shame on the dolt would be go - ing, Nor - tar - ry for one bot - tle more!

CHORUS

Come fill, fill, my good fel - low! Fill high, high, my good fel - low! And

let's be mer - ry and mel - low, And let us have one bot - tle more!

1. Come fill, fill, my good fellow!
   Fill high, high, my good fellow!
   And let's be merry and mellow,
   And let us have one bottle more.
   When warm the heart is flowing,
   And bright the fancy glowing,
   Oh! shame on the dolt would be going,
   Nor tarry for one bottle more!

CHORUS: Come fill, fill, my good fellow!
         Fill high, high, my good fellow!
         And let's be merry and mellow,
         And let us have one bottle more!

2. My heart let me but lighten,
   And life let me but brighten,
   And care let me but frighten,
   He'll fly us with one bottle more!
   By day, tho' he confound me,
   When friends by night have found me,
   There is Paradise around me,
   But let me have one bottle more! *Chorus:*

3. So now, here's to the lasses!
   See, see, while the toast passes,
   How it lights up beaming glasses!
   Encore to the lasses, encore.
   We'll toast the welcome greeting
   Of hearts in union beating,
   And oh! for our next merry meeting,
   Huzzah! then for one bottle more! *Chorus:*

THREE GUDE FELLOWS
ROBERT BURNS

CHORUS: There's three true gude fellows,   (. . . *good fellows*)
         There's three true gude fellows,
         There's three true gude fellows,
            Down ayont yon glen!   (. . . *beyond* . . .)

It's now the day is dawin,   (. . . *dawning*)
But or night do fa' in,   (*But ere night* . . .)
Whase cock's best at crawin,   (*Whose cock's best at crowing*)
Willie, thou sall ken!   (. . . *shall know*)

THE TOWN DRUMMER

CHORUS: Aye drummin' an' ruffin',
               Aye soakin' an' scuffin',
               Aye jokin' and stuffin',
                  Ken ye Tam an' his drum?   *(Do you know . . .)*

1. I trow he's a stuffy wee cricket,
    Though cruikit, wee-boukit, an' stickit,   *(. . . crooked, small-bodied and stooped)*
    He's no very easily lickit,   *(. . . licked or beaten)*
        Stuffy wee Tam an' his drum.
    Whaure'er maut or mischief is brewin',   *(. . . malt . . .)*
    Whaure'er there is aught to get fou on,   *(. . . drunk . . .)*
    Whaure'er there is onything new in,
        You're sure to meet Tam an his' drum. *Chorus:*

2. A' sleepy new-married folks, scornin'
    To rise up betimes in the mornin',
    Gie Tammie his fee an' his warnin',
        He's sure to be there wi' his drum.
    The bride in a flusterin' flurry,
    The bridegroom a' foamin' wi' fury,
    He bangs on his claes in a hurry,   *(. . . clothes . . .)*
        An' curses baith Tam an' his drum. *Chorus:* *(. . . both . . .)*

3. At twalhours, when knee-breekit carles   *(. . . knee-breeched old men)*
    Slip in to their whisky an' farles,
    Gin Tammie has gotten his earles,
        He's sure to be there wi' his drum.
    At ilka puir bodie's cross roupin',   *(At every poor body's . . . coughing)*
    At ilka bit niffer or coupin',   *(At every exchange or barter)*
    The moment ye ca' the gill-stoup in,
        You're sure to see Tam an' his drum. *Chorus:*

4. At e'enin', when ten o'clock's chappin',   *(. . . striking)*
    An' wark-folk a' homeward are stappin',   *(. . . stepping)*
    Straught up the High Street he comes pappin', *(Straight . . . popping)*
        An' shuts a' the shops wi' his drum.
    At midnicht, when bodies get bouzie,   *(boozy)*
    An' set up in flames their bit housie,
    Wee Tammie, half-naked an' tousie,   *(. . . shaggy)*
        Awaukens the town wi' his drum. *Chorus:*

5. When our Bailies, wi' round chubby faces,
   Are coach'd down in state to the races,
   A' the horses show aff their best paces,
      At tuck o' wee Tam an' his drum.
   I trow he is merry an' cheery,
   Wi' Tammie ye canna weel weary,
   But a' wad gang heeligoleery,   (. . . *all would go crazy*)
      Gin ye wanted wee Tam an' his drum.

from: *One Hundred Songs* by James Ballantine; John S. Marr, Glasgow, 1866

Come Fill, Fill, My Good Fellow

This drinking song has, in common with much Scottish and Irish dance music, a melodic pattern that shifts from the tonic triad to the sub-tonic, a triad a whole step below, and then back again:

Going directly in parallel motion from one triad to the next was forbidden according to the catechism of harmony in the Classic era. We find Beethoven, in keeping with this tradition of concert music, avoiding parallel intervals of fifths and octaves by inserting a modulating chord [C^7] [D^7].

Three Gude Fellows

In the commentary for this song, which is in the *Scots Musical Museum* (1796), it is stated that Burns hastily wrote the four-line verse at the publisher's request so that the tune could be included in the book. Both James Johnson, the editor, and Burns greatly admired the melody, but only the words to the chorus were known. In a letter to Alexander Cunningham on May 4, 1789, Burns wrote: "I have a good mind to write verses on you all" [his friends, Cruikshank, Dunbar, and Cunningham—*ed.*] "to the tune of 'Three gude fellows ayont the glen.' "

In Ballantine's *One Hundred Songs* (1866) this one is listed as derived from the air "Three Gude Fellows." The town drummer was a type of wait, a special musician whose occupation went back to medieval times. These were the watchmen, the town criers, town pipers, whose function was to announce the hours. The duties were at times broadened to include music for welcoming ceremonies and special occasions such as the races mentioned in the last verse of this song.

25

FOR THE SAKE O' SOMEBODY

ROBERT BURNS (1759–1796)　　　　　　　　JOHANN NEPOMUK HUMMEL (1778–1837)

Andantino amoroso con moto

heart is sair, I dare na tell, My heart is sair for
powers that smile on vir - tuous love, O, sweet - ly smile on

Some - bod - y; I could wake a win - ter night____
Some - bod - y! Frae il - ka dan - ger keep him free, And

MUSIC AND TEXT SOURCE: G. Thomson.

1. My heart is sair___I darena tell,___   (*sore . . . dare not*)
   My heart is sair for Somebody;
   I could wake a winter night
   For the sake o' Somebody.
           O-hon! for Somebody!   (*Alack!*)
           O-hey! for Somebody!   (*Alas!*)
   I could range the world around
   For the sake o' Somebody.

2. Ye Powers that smile on virtuous love,
   O, sweetly smile on Somebody!
   Frae ilka danger keep him free,   (*From any . . .*)
   And send me safe my Somebody.
           O-hon! for Somebody!
           O-hey! for Somebody!
   I wad do___what wad I not?___   (*. . . would . . .*)
   For the sake o' Somebody!

Burns took the chorus of a song with this title from Ramsay's *Tea-Table Miscellany* (1724–1727) and built his poem upon it. The indefinite "Somebody" was really quite definite among the Jacobites; it was an allusion to Prince Charles, the Scottish claimant to the throne. This is illustrated in a verse from one of the Jacobite song collections:

If Somebody were come again,
Then Somebody maun cross the main;   (*. . . must cross . . .*)
And ilka ane will get his ain,   (*And every one will get his own*)
And I will see my Somebody.

Burns had difficulty writing lyrics to the tune, as first printed in *Scots Musical Museum* (1787–1803). He wrote to the editor: "The notation of the music seems incorrect, but I send it as I got it."

He recommended to the attention of James Johnson, the editor, an earlier tune in the *Caledonian Pocket Companion* (1752). This is the one, as amended by Peter Urbani in *A Selection of Scots Songs* (1793–1799), that is more generally known. It is this version that is printed above.

One can't help noticing the affinity of phrases of the tune and even of the text with Burns' "Gin a body meet a body, Comin' thro' the rye" and also with "Auld Lang Syne."

26

PIBROCH OF DONUIL DHU

SIR WALTER SCOTT (1771–1832)   JOHANN NEPOMUK HUMMEL (1778–1837)

Pi - broch of Do - nuil Dhu, Pi - broch of Do - nuil, Wake thy wild voice a - new,

Sum - mon Clan Co - nuil. Come a - way, come a - way, Hark to the sum - mons!

MUSIC AND TEXT SOURCE: G. Thomson.

Come in your war ar - ray, Gen - tles and com - mons.

CHORUS

Come a - way, come a - way, Hark to the sum - mons Come in your war ar - ray,

Gen - tles and com - mons.

1. Pibroch of Donuil Dhu,   *(Bagpipe call . . .)*
   Pibroch of Donuil,
   Wake thy wild voice anew,
   Summon Clan Conuil.   *(Clan Council)*
   Come away, come away,
   Hark to the summons!
   Come in your war array,
   Gentles and commons.

CHORUS: Come away, come away,
           Hark to the summons
           Come in your war array,
           Gentles and commons.

2. Come from deep glen, and
   From mountain so rocky,
   The war pipe and pennon
   Are at Inverlochy:
   Come every hill-plaid, and
   True heart that wears one,
   Come every steel blade, and
   Strong hand that bears one. *Chorus:*

3. Leave untended the herd,
   The flock without shelter;
   Leave the corpse uninterr'd,
   The bride at the alter;
   Leave the deer, leave the steer,
   Leave nets and barges;
   Come with your fighting gear,
   Broadswords and targes. *Chorus:*

4. Come as the winds come, when
   Forests are rended;
   Come as the waves come, when
   Navies are stranded;
   Faster come, faster come,
   Faster and faster,
   Chief, vassal, page, and groom,
   Tenant and master. *Chorus:*

5. Fast they come, fast they come;
   See how they gather!
   Wide waves the eagle plume,
   Blended with heather.
   Cast your plaids, draw your blades,
   Forward each man set;
   Pibroch of Donuil Dhu,
   Knell for the onset! *Chorus:*

The pibroch is the popularized form of the Gaelic word "piobaireachd." It is the name given a special variation form of bagpipe music, of which there are three main types: the salute, the gathering, and the lament. "The Pibroch of Donuil Dhu," subtitled in Thomson "The Pipe Summons of Donald the Black," refers to the battle at Inverlochy in 1431, in which Donald Balloch defeated the Earl of Mar and Earl of Caithness. The tune was long known as "Lochiel's March." The poem was written by Sir Walter Scott in 1816.

The arrangement by Hummel was written in 1830, but was not printed until 1841.

27

TRUE-HEARTED WAS HE
THE SAD SWAIN

ROBERT BURNS (1759–1796)　　　　　　CARL MARIA VON WEBER (1786–1826)

1. True-heart-ed was he the sad swain o' the Yar-row, And
2. (Oh) Fresh is the rose in the gay dew-y morn-ing, And

fair are the maids on the banks of the _ Ayr; But by the sweet side of the
sweet is the lil-y at eve-ning _ close; But in the fair pre-sence o'

MUSIC AND TEXT SOURCE: G. Thomson.

Nith's wind-ing riv - er, Are lov - ers as faith - ful, and maid - ens as __ fair.
love - ly young Jes - sie, Un - seen is the lil - y, un - heed - ed the __ rose.

Cello

To e - qual young Jes - sie seek Sco - tia all o - ver: To
Love sits in her smile, _____ a wiz - ard en - snar - ing; En -

e - qual young Jes - sie you seek it in __ vain; Grace beau - ty and el - e - gance
thron'd in her een he de - liv - ers his __ law; And still to her charms she a -

fet - ter her lov - er, And maid - en - ly mod - es - ty fix - es the __ chain.
lone is a strang - er; Her mod - est de - mean - our's the jew - el of __ a'!

Vln.   Piano   Fl.

ff   f   pp

Cello.

1. True-hearted was he the sad swain o' the Yarrow,
   And fair are the maids on the banks of the Ayr;
   But by the sweet side of the Nith's winding river,
   Are lovers as faithful, and maidens as fair.
   To equal young Jessie, seek Scotia all over:
   To equal young Jessie, you seek it in vain;
   Grace, beauty, and elegance fetter her lover,
   And maidenly modesty fixes the chain.

2. [Oh!] Fresh is the rose in the gay dewy morning,
   And sweet is the lily at evening close;
   But in the fair presence o' lovely young Jessie,
   Unseen is the lily, unheeded the rose.
   Love sits in her smile, a wizard ensnaring;
   Enthron'd in her een he delivers his law:
   And still to her charms she alone is a stranger;
   Her modest demeanour's the jewel of a'!

Burns wrote this poem for Thomson's *Scottish Airs* in 1793. The model for his description was Miss Jessie Staig of Dumfries. Burns would not make a change in a line as suggested by Thomson, contending that, though it would improve a stiff line, "it would spoil the likeness, so the picture must stand."

The poem is set to the tune of "Bonny Dundee," or "Adieu Dundee" as it is also known. The tune was first notated in the Skene Manuscript (*c.* 1630).

28

JOHN ANDERSON MY JO

ROBERT BURNS (1759–1796)   CARL MARIA VON WEBER (1786–1826)

Andantino

1. John An - der - son my jo, John, When__ we were first ac -
2. John An - der - son my jo, John, We__ clamb the hill the -

quent, Your locks were like the ra - ven, Your
gith - er; And mon - y a can - tie day, John, We've

bon - nie brow was brent. But now your brow is beld, John, Your
had wi' ane an - ith-er: Now we maun tot - ter down, John, And

locks are like the snaw, But __ bless - ings on your
hand in hand we'll go, And __ sleep the - gith - er

frost - y pow, John An - der - son, my jo!
at the foot, John An - der - son, my jo!

Cello

Cello

1. John Anderson my jo, John,   *(. . . my sweetheart, . . .)*
   When we were first acquent,   *(. . . acquainted)*
   Your locks were like the raven,
   Your bonnie brow was brent;   *(. . . unwrinkled, smooth)*
   But now your brow is beld, John,   *(. . . bald)*
   Your locks are like the snaw,   *(. . . snow)*
   But blessings on your frosty pow,   *(. . . head)*
   John Anderson my jo!

2. John Anderson my jo, John,
   We clamb the hill thegither;   *(. . . together)*
   And mony a cantie day, John,   *(. . . many a merry . . .)*
   We've had wi' ane anither: *(. . . with one another)*
   Now we maun totter down, John,   *(. . . must . . .)*
   And hand in hand we'll go,
   And sleep thegither at the foot,
   John Anderson my jo!

"Jo" is the Scottish term for sweetheart. Burns's poem "John Anderson my jo" was first printed in *Scots Musical Museum* in 1790. It is based on an old song which goes:

John Anderson my jo, John,
I wonder what you meen,
To lie sae lang i' the mornin'   *(To lie so long . . .)*
And sit sae late at e'en.
Ye'll blear a' your e'en, John,   *(You'll get bleary-eyed . . .)*
And why do ye so?
Come sooner to your bed at e'en,
John Anderson my jo.

Compared with the tender sentiments expressed in Burns's lyrics, this text portrays a more mundane marriage. In a version in Percy's *Reliques* (1765), there is further marital discord and even infidelity:

WOMAN
John Anderson my jo,
Cum in as ze gae bye,
And ze sall get a sheip's heid   *(. . . sheep's head)*
Weel baken in a pye;   *(Well baked in a pie)*
Weel baken in a pye,
And the haggis in a pat;   *(pudding boiled with sheep's or cow's guts)*
John Anderson my jo,
Cum in and ze's get that.

MAN
And how doe ze, Cummer?   *(How are you, woman)*
And how hae ze threven?   *(. . . have you thrived)*
And how mony bairns hae ze?   *(. . . how many children . . .)*

WOMAN

Cummer, I hae seven.

MAN

Are they to zour awin gude man?   (. . . *to your own master*)

WOMAN

Na, Cummer, na;

For five of tham were gotten

Quhan he was awa'.   (*When he was away*)

Percy, in his notes on this song, discusses the question of its derivation from a hymn tune of the Catholic service:

It is a received tradition in Scotland that at the time of the Reformation ridiculous and obscene songs were composed to be sung by the rabble to the tunes of the most favourite hymns in the Latin Service. "Greensleeves and pudding pies," . . . "Maggie Lauder" was another and "John Anderson my jo" was a third. The original music of all these burlesque sonnets was very fine.

J. C. Dick in *The Songs of Robert Burns* takes issue:

It is ridiculous to speak of the very fine original music of these "sonnets" in the past tense. All were very popular and well known in Percy's time, and they are well known now, as secular folk tunes with secular words. What was done in Scotland was to imitate every European country including England. Religious parodies of secular songs were written for popular secular airs and these "sangs," mixed up with hymns and psalms, are preserved in the collection known as *The Gude and Godlie Ballads*.

In another opinion, Dr. Burney states:

Though the Reformation has banished superstition from the land, fragments of canto fermo, like rags of Popery, still remained in our old secular tunes and continue to have admission in the new.

One might conclude in this controversy that the traffic in tunes went in both directions.

The earliest notation of the song is in the Skene Manuscript (c. 1630). It is similar to the English "I am the Duke of Norfolk," the Irish "The Cruiskeen Lawn" ("The Little Jug"), and the Welsh "Yn Nyffryn Clwyd" ("The Vale of Clyde").

29

WHERE HA'E YE BEEN A' THE DAY?

HECTOR MACNEILL (1746–1818)   CARL MARIA VON WEBER (1786–1826)

Where ha'e ye been a' the day, My ___ boy ___ Tam - mie?

Where ha'e ye been a' the day, My ___ boy ___ Tam - mie?

MUSIC AND TEXT SOURCE: G. Thomson.

I've been by burn and flow - 'ry brae, Mead - ow green and moun - tain grey,

Court - ing o' this young thing just come frae her mam - mie.

Fl.

Vln.

Cello

D. S. %

1. Where ha'e ye been a' the day,
   My boy Tammie? } bis
   I've been by burn and flow'ry brae,
   Meadow green an' mountain grey,
   Courting o' this young thing
   Just come frae her mammie.

   (Where have . . . all . . .)

   (. . . brook and flowery slope)

   (. . . from her mother)

2. Whaur' gat ye that young thing,
   My boy Tammie? } bis
   I got her down in yonder howe,
   Smiling on a broomie knowe,
   Herding ae wee lamb and ewe,
   For her puir mammie.

   (Where got . . .)

   (. . . hollow or dell)
   (. . . scrubby hillock)

   (. . . poor . . .)

3. What said ye to the bonnie bairn,
   My boy Tammie? } bis
   I praised her een, sae lovely blue,
   Her dimpled cheek and cherry mou';
   An' pree'd it aft; as ye may trow!—
   She said she'd tell her mammie.

   (. . . cherry mouth)
   (. . . tasted it often . . .)

4. I held her to my beatin' heart,
   My young, my smiling lammie! } bis
   I hae a house, it cost me dear,
   I've wealth o' plenishin' and gear;
   Ye'se get it a', were't ten times mair,
   Gin ye will leave your mammie.

   (. . . furnishings . . .)
   (Ye shall get it, . . . more)
   (If . . .)

5. The smile gaed aff her bonnie face—
   I maunna leave my mammie. } bis
   She's gi'en me meat, she's gi'en me claes,
   She's been my comfort a' my days:—
   My father's death brought mony waes!
   I canna leave my mammie.

   (. . . smile left her . . .)
   (. . . must not . . .)
   (. . . given . . . clothes)

   (. . . many woes)
   (. . . cannot . . .)

6. We'll tak' her hame and mak' her fain,
   My ain kind-hearted lammie. } bis
   We'll gi'e her meat, we'll gi'e her claes,
   We'll be her comfort a' her days.
   The wee thing gi'es her hand, and says,
   There! gang and ask my mammie.

   (. . . home and make her inclined to consent)

   (. . . go . . .)

7. Has she been to the kirk wi' thee,
   My boy Tammie? } bis
   She has been to the kirk wi' me,
   An' the tear was in her e'e:
   For O! she's but a young thing,
   Just come frae her mammie.

   (. . . church . . .)

   (. . . eye)

144

The verses by Hector Macneill were first printed in *The Bee* (1791) and were first published together with the tune in Napier's collection in 1792. The song text is probably the ancestor of a group of songs known as "Billy Boy," including the popular American version, which goes:

> Oh, where have you been, Billy Boy, Billy Boy,
> Oh, where have you been, charming Billy,
> I have been to seek a wife,
> She's the joy of my life,
> She's a young thing and cannot leave her mother.

30

HEY TUTTI, TAITI

(Scots Wha Hae wi' Wallace Bled)

ROBERT BURNS (1759–1796)   MAX BRUCH (1838–1920)

Allegro energico

TENOR SOLO

1. Land - la - dy, count the law - in, The day is near the daw - in;
2. Cog, and ye were ay fou, Cog, and ye were ay fou,
3. Weel may we a' be! Ill may we nev - er see!

Ye're a' blind drunk, boys, And I'm but jol - ly fou.
I wad sit and sing to you, If ye were ay fou.
God bless the king And the com - pa - nie!

sempre arp.

CHORUS

Hey tut - ti tai - ti, Hey tut - ti, tai - ti,

MUSIC AND TEXT SOURCE: Max Bruch, *Zwölf schottische Volkslieder, bearbeitet.*

How ___ tut - ti, tai - ti, ___ Hey ___ tut - ti tai - ti, ___

CHORUS

Wha's ___ fou ___ now? Hey tut - ti, tai - ti,

Hey tut - ti, tai - ti, How ___ tut - ti, tai - ti, ___

Hey ___ tut - ti, tai - ti, ___ Wha's ___ fou ___ now?

col 8.

1. Landlady, count the lawin,   (. . . bill)
   The day is near the dawin;   (. . . dawning)
   Ye're a' blind drunk, boys,   (You're all . . .)
   And I'm but jolly fou.   (. . . tipsy)

CHORUS: Hey tutti, taiti,
          How tutti, taiti,
          Hey tutti, taiti,
          Wha's fou now?   (Who's drunk, now?)

2. Cog, and ye were ay fou,   (Bumpers [Glasses], . . .)
   Cog, and ye were ay fou,
   I wad sit and sing to you,   (I would . . .)
   If ye were ay fou! *Chorus:*

3. Weel may we a' be!
   Ill may we never see!
   God bless the king
   And the companie! *Chorus:*

SCOTS, WHA HAE WI' WALLACE BLED

ROBERT BURNS

1. Scots, wha hae wi' Wallace bled,   (. . . who have with . . .)
   Scots, wham Bruce has aften led,   (. . . whom . . .)
   Welcome to your gory bed
   Or to victorie!

   Now's the day, and now's the hour:
   See the front o' battle lour,   (. . . lowering [impending])
   See approach proud Edward's power—
   Chains and slaverie!

2. Wha will be a traitor knave?
   Wha can fill a coward's grave?
   Wha so base as be a slave?—
   Let him turn, and flee!

   Wha for Scotland's king and law
   Freedom's sword will strongly draw,
   Freeman stand or freeman fa',
   Let him follow me!

3. By oppression's woes and pains,
   By your sons in servile chains,
   We will drain our dearest veins
   But they shall be free!

Lay the proud usurpers low!
Tyrants fall in every foe!
Liberty's in every blow!—
Let us do, or die!

Hey Tutti, Taiti

The tune and poem in *Scots Musical Museum* (1787–1803) do not contain the repeated first line of the chorus as in Bruch's arrangement. On the same page in this source, there is a Jacobite song of the early eighteenth century from which Burns derived the refrain, "Hey tutti, taiti":

When you hear the trumpet sounds
Tutti taitie to the drum,
Up your swords and down your guns,
And to the louns again.   (*And at the rascals again*)

CHORUS: Fill up your bunkers high,
               We'll drink a' your barrels dry,
               Out upon them, fy! fy!
               That winna do't again.   (*That will not do it again*)

Max Bruch quotes this tune repeatedly as a main theme in the Finale of his *Scottish Fantasy* for solo violin and orchestra.

Scots Wha Hae wi' Wallace Bled

This is a variant of "Hey Tutti, Taiti." In a letter to George Thomson dated September 1, 1793, Burns enclosed a copy of his new poem with some interesting observations concerning folk songs:

My dear Sir, You know that my pretensions to musical taste are merely a few of nature's instincts, untaught and untutored by art. For this reason, many musical compositions, particularly where much of the merit lies in counterpoint, however they may ravish the ears of you connoisseurs, affect my simple lug [ear] no otherwise than merely as melodious din. On the other hand, by way of amends, I am delighted with many little melodies, which the learned musician despises as silly and insipid. I do not know whether the old air *Hey Tutti, Taiti* may rank among this number; but well I know that with Fraser's hautboy it has often filled my eyes with tears. There is a tradition which I have met in many places in Scotland, that it was Robert Bruce's march at Bannockburn. This thought, in my yesternight's evening walk, warmed me to a pitch of enthusiasm on the theme of liberty and independence, which I threw into a kind of Scots Ode, that one might suppose to be the gallant royal Scot's address to his heroic followers on that eventful morning. So may God ever defend the cause of Truth and Liberty as he did that day. Amen!

P.S. I shewed the air to Urbani, who was highly pleased with it and begged me to make soft verses for it; but I had no idea of giving myself any trouble on the subject, till the accidental recollection of that glorious struggle for Freedom, associated with the glowing ideas of other struggles of the same nature, *not quite so ancient,* roused my rhyming mania. Clarke's set of the tune, with his bass, you will find in the Museum, though I am afraid that the air is not what will entitle it to a place in your elegant selection.

Burns' fears were well grounded, for Thomson and a committee declared the tune to be unacceptable, and prevailed upon Burns to alter his verses, which they liked, to fit another tune, "Lewie Gordon." When still further changes were requested, Burns sent Thomson the following ultimatum: "My Ode pleases me so much, that I cannot alter it. Your proposed alterations would, in my opinion, make it tame. I am exceedingly obliged to you for putting me on reconstructing it, as I think I have much improved it. . . . I have scrutinised it over and over; and to the world some way or other, it shall go as it is."

Thomson printed the text with the "Lewis Gordon" tune in 1799, three years after Burns' death. Upon learning of this situation, the poet's public forced Thomson to admit his error and to reprint in 1801 the poem with the tune Burns originally had in mind.

Thomson's *Scottish Airs* 1801

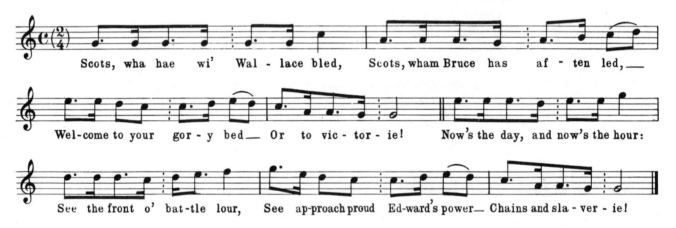

31

LORD GREGORY

(*Oh, Mirk, Mirk Is This Midnight Hour*)

MAX BRUCH (1838–1920)

Andante sostenuto

1. "Oh, o - pen the door Lord Greg - o - ry, Oh,

o - pen and let me in; The rain rains on my

scar - let robes, The dew drops o'er my chin."

MUSIC SOURCE: Max Bruch, *Zwölf schottische Volkslieder, bearbeitet.*
TEXT SOURCE: *Scots Musical Museum* and Francis J. Child, *The English and Scottish Popular Ballads,* 1882–98; Houghton Mifflin & Co., Boston, 1904; reprint: Dover Publications, 1965.

"If you are the lass that I ____ loved once, ____ As I trow you ____ are _____ not she, ____ Come give me ___ some of the to - kens That ___ passed ___ be - tween you and me."

1. "Oh, open the door, Lord Gregory,
    Oh, open and let me in;
    The rain rains on my scarlet robes,
    The dew drops o'er my chin."
    "If you are the lass that I loved once,
    As I trow you are not she,
    Come give me some of the tokens
    That passed between you and me."

2. "Have you not mind, Lord Gregory,
    Since we sat at the wine,
    When we changed the rings of our fingers
    And ay the worst fell mine?
    Mine was of the massy gold,
    And thine was of the tin;
    Mine was true and trusty both,
    And thine was false within."

3. "If you be the lass of Roch Royall,
    As I trow you not to be,
    You will tell me some other love-token
    That was betwixt you and me."
    "But open the door now, Lord Gregory,
    Oh, open the door I pray,
    For your young son that is in my arms
    Will be dead ere it be day."

4. "Awa, awa, ye ill woman,   (*Away . . .*)
    For here ye sha' no' win in;   (*For here you shall not enter*)
    Gae drown ye in the raging sea,   (*Go . . .*)
    Or hang on the gallows pin."
    "Ah, wae be to you, Lord Gregory,   (*. . . woe . . .*)
    Ah, ill death may you die!
    You will not be the death of one,
    But ye'll be the death of three!"

OH, MIRK, MIRK IS THIS MIDNIGHT HOUR

ROBERT BURNS

1. O, mirk, mirk is this midnight hour,   (*O, dark, . . .*)
    And loud the tempest's roar;
    A waefu' wanderer seeks the tower—
    Lord Gregory, ope thy door!
    An exile frae her father's ha',   (*. . . hall*)
    And a' for the sake o' thee,
    At least some pity on me shaw,   (*. . . show*)
    If love it may na be.   (*. . . not be*)

2. Lord Gregory, mind'st thou not the grove
   By bonie Irwin side,
   Where first I own'd that virgin love
   I lang, lang had denied?
   How aften didst thou pledge and vow,   (. . . *often* . . .)
   Thou wad for ay be mine!   (. . . *would* . . .)
   And my fond heart, itsel sae true,   (. . . *so* . . .)
   It ne'er mistrusted thine.

3. Hard is thy heart, Lord Gregory,
   And flinty is thy breast:
   Thou bolt of heaven that flashed by,
   O, wilt thou bring me rest!
   Ye mustering thunders from above,
   Your willing victim see,
   But spare and pardon my fause love   (. . . *false* . . .)
   His wrangs to Heaven and me!

Lord Gregory

As "The Bonny Lass o' Lochroyan" the text first appeared in Herd's *Scottish Songs* in 1776, and the tune was first printed in *Scots Musical Museum* in 1787. According to Burns, the ballad's locale is Lochroyan in Galloway. In the Child collection it is listed as "The Lass of Roch Royal," where the ballad contains thirty-five verses.

O, Mirk, Mirk Is This Midnight Hour

Burns wrote these verses, based on the "Lord Gregory" ballad, for Thomson's *Scottish Airs,* 1798.

32

SAW YE MY FATHER?

MAX BRUCH (1838–1920)

1. Oh, saw ye my fa - ther, or saw ye my mith - er, Or
2. It's now ten at night, an' the stars gi'e nae light, An' the

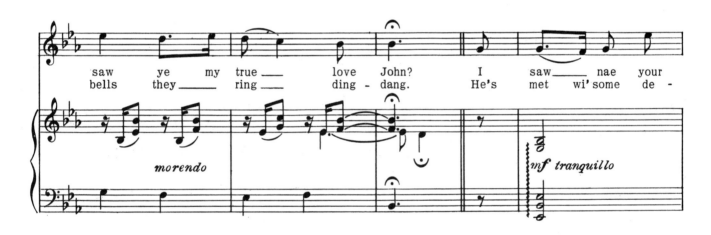

saw ye my true love John? I saw nae your
bells they ring ding - dang. He's met wi' some de -

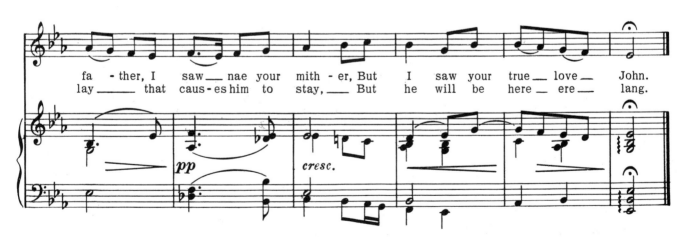

fa - ther, I saw nae your mith - er, But I saw your true love John.
lay that caus - es him to stay, But he will be here ere lang.

MUSIC AND TEXT SOURCE: *Max Bruch, Zwölf schottische Volkslieder, bearbeitet.*

1. Oh, saw ye my father, or saw ye my mither,   (. . . *mother*)
    Or saw ye my true love John?
  I saw nae your father, I saw nae your mither,   (. . . *not* . . .)
    But I saw your true love John.

2. It's now ten at night, an' the stars gi'e nae light,   (. . . *give no* . . .)
    An' the bells they ring ding-dang,
  He's met wi' some delay that causes him to stay,
    But he will be here ere lang.   (. . . *long*)

3. The surly auld carle did naething but snarl,   (. . . *old peasant did*
    An' Johnny's face it grew red,   *nothing* . . .)
  Yet tho' he often sigh'd, he ne'er a word replied,
    Till a' were asleep in bed.

4. Then up Johnny rose, an' to the door he goes,
    An' gently tirl'd at the pin,   (. . . *rattled the door-latch*)
  The lassie takin' tent, unto the door she went,   (. . . *taking heed* . . .)
    An' she open'd an' lat him in.   (. . . *let* . . .)

5. An' are ye come at last! an' do I hold you fast!
    An' is my Johnny true!
  I have nae time to tell, but sae lang's I like mysel,
    Sae lang shall I like you.

6. Flee up, flee up, my bonnie grey cock,
    An' craw when it is day;   (. . . *crow* . . .)
  An' your neck shall be like the bonnie beaten gold,
    An' your wings of the silver grey.

7. The cock proved false, an' untrue he was,
    For he crew an hour owre soon: (. . . *over soon, early*)
  The lassie thocht it day when she sent her love away,   (. . . *thought* . . .)
    An' it was but a blink o' the moon.

The text was first printed in David Herd's *The Ancient and Modern Scots Songs* in 1769 and was first combined with the tune in Neil Stewart's *Thirty Scots Songs* in 1772. Robert Burns, one year later, wrote to George Thomson:

"Saw ye my father?" is one of my greatest favourites. The evening before last I wandered out, and began a tender song in what I think is its native style. . . . Every country girl sings "Saw ye my father?"

Burns' song is printed in *Scots Musical Museum* (1787) and in the Thomson Collection as "Where are the joys I had met in the morning?"

    The simple but artful setting by Bruch contrasts the two sections of the song. By arpeggiating the accompaniment in the first part and sustaining the chords in the second section the dialogue form of the verses are underscored.

IV

WELSH SONGS

Despite its proximity to England, Wales has tenaciously maintained its language and its own traditional music. Wales is especially noted for its harp music tradition, which, it is surmised, goes back to ancient times. This is difficult to ascertain because, until 1742 with the first publication of some Welsh airs, no music had been recorded. However, we do know from Pepys' diary in 1666 that Welsh harpers were famed in London, and we learn of "Evens, the famous man upon the harp, having not his equal in the world." Most of the well-known national songs have come from the harp melodies, while the folk songs of the unaccompanied vocal tradition have been neglected. The harp airs were generally instrumental by nature rather than of vocal melodic shape. According to W. S. Gwynn Williams in *Welsh National Music and Dance,* 1932, many have been performed in conjunction with pennillion singing, through which process the melodies became somewhat simplified and more vocal. In N. Bennett's *Collection of Old Welsh Airs* (1896) pennillion singing is defined and described as follows:

The literal meaning of the word "pennill"—of which "pennillion" is the plural—is a stanza; and Pennillion singing means the singing of stanzas to the accompaniment of an instrument, under certain rules and regulations. The singer must not only not sing the melody—except occasional notes, and these chiefly cadential—but he must neither start with it, nor on the first beat of the bar, or musical measure . . . the strictly defined melody being allotted to the instrument.

The instrument was understood to be the harp. These rules were observed during great festivals, "Eisteddfodau," where contests were held in which bards competed. There are accounts of these gatherings from the sixth century, continuing until today when they have taken on the character of choral festivals.

There are two types of pennillion: the one from North Wales is closer to the solo extempore bardic style; while the South Wales style is more group activity in which each member improvises a single verse alternating with choral "fa-la-la" refrains, something in the manner of "Deck the Halls."

Haydn arranged forty-one and Beethoven twenty-six of the Welsh songs contained in Thomson's collection.

33

AWAY TO THE OAKEN GROVE

(Hob y Derri Danno)

ANNE HUNTER (C. 1800)   JOSEF HAYDN (1732–1809)

Vivace

1. Sweet, how sweet the haw-thorn bloom-ing, Fa la la la la la   la la
2. Un-waith et - o mi ddy-wed - af Hob y der-ri dan - no, Sian, fwyn

la,   'Round the balm - y air per-fum-ing, Fa la la la la la   la
Sian?   Nid oes tes a r am-ser gau-af Dyn-a ga-nu et o, Sian, fwyn

MUSIC AND ENGLISH TEXT SOURCE: G. Thomson.

la,

Sian.

Love-ly May these are thy trea-sures, Fa la la la la

Ond mae Sian yn wrth he-neidd-io, Dal di syl-w Sian.

In thy train at-tend the pleas-ures, Fa la la la la la la,

E - fo car-iad - yn gwe freidd-io: Sian fwyn, turd i'r llwyn,

These thy treas-ures love-ly May (Fa la la.)

Sein-iaf en-w Sia-ni fwyn, Sian, fwyn Sian.

1. Sweet, how sweet the hawthorn blooming,
   Fa la la la la la la la la,
   'Round the balmy air perfuming,
   Fa la la la la la la la la,
   Lovely May, these are thy treasures,
   Fa la la la la,
   In thy train attend the pleasures,
   Fa la la la la la la,
   These thy treasures, lovely May,
   (Fa la la).

HOB Y DERRI DANNO (JANE, SWEET JANE)

TALHAIARN

Unwaith eto mi ddywedaf
Hob y derri danno, Sian, fwyn Sian?
Nid oes tes ar amser gauaf
Dyna ganu et o, Sian, fwyn Sian.
Ond mae Sian yn wrth heneiddio,
Dal di sylw Sian.
Efo cariadyn gwe freiddio:
Sian fwyn, turd i'r llwyn,
Seiniaf enw Siani fwyn, Sian, fwyn Sian.

1. Joy upon thy bright cheek dances,
   Hob y derri danno, Jane, sweet Jane;
   From thine eye love's arrow glances,
   Hob y derri danno, Jane, sweet Jane!
   In the greenwood I am waiting,
   All alone, sweet Jane;
   To the tuneful birds relating
   How I love thee, Jane;
   Come unto thy trysting tree, Jane, sweet Jane.

2. Oh! that winged were thy lover,
   Hob y derri danno, Jane, sweet Jane!
   Round thee like a dove to hover,
   Hob y derri danno, Jane, sweet Jane!
   Think not I can ever leave thee,
   No! the thought is vain!
   Think not I can e'er deceive thee;
   Oh! no! pretty Jane!
   Thou art all the world to me,
   Jane, sweet, Jane!

from: Thomas' *Welsh Melodies,* translation by Oliphant

The English text for the song as printed in Thomson's collection is by Mrs. Hunter, the wife of John Hunter, the surgeon who was a friend of Haydn. In that edition, the vocal line ends two measures short of the actual end of the melody, which continues in the piano part. The missing notes have been added in small notes together with another phrase of "Fa la la" necessary to complete the text. The Welsh refrain, "Hob y derri danno" is quite similar to the English "Hey derry down O." There are two different Welsh tunes to the text; the one in this book is from North Wales.

34

HUNTING THE HARE

(Hela'r 'Sgyfarnog)

JOSEF HAYDN (1732–1809)

Allegretto scherzoso

Hence a - way — with i - dle sor - row,
Awn i hel - a'r 'sg - yf - arn - og.

Bane of life's — un - cer - tain hour; Few the joys — from
Dym - a for - eu hyf - ryd iach; Cod - wyd hi — ar

time we bor - row, Hold them while — with - in — your pow'r.
graig eith - in - og: Hei! y cwn — a'r gw - ta fach!

MUSIC AND TEXT SOURCE: G. Thomson.

Hunt ___ the hare ___ o'er hills ___ and val - leys, Cheer - ful wake ___ the
Fel ___ y gwynt, ___ neu'n gynt ___ na hy - ny, Gyd - a'r cwn ___ a

ris - ing morn; _____ When she from ___ her
hith - au'r awn; _____ Ar y ffridd ___ wrth

cham - ber sal - lies, Greet her with ___ the ear - ly horn.
fyn'd i fyn - y, Dy - na i - ddi dro - fa iawn.

1. Hence away with idle sorrow,
   Bane of life's uncertain hour;
   Few the joys from time we borrow,
   Hold them while within your pow'r.
   Hunt the hare o'er hills and valleys,
   Cheerful wake the rising morn;
   When she from her chamber sallies,
   Greet her with the early horn.

2. Health and peace and spirits gaily
   Temper'd by the buxom air:
   While such blessings court you daily,
   Why prefer dull, pining care?
   Hunt the hare o'er hills and valleys,
   Cheerful wake the rising morn,
   When she from her chamber sallies,
   Greet her with the early horn.

3. Then, when fast the sun descending
   Seeks his chambers in the west,
   Hasten where good cheer attending
   Waits to welcome ev'ry guest,
   While the goblet gaily quaffing
   Round and round you hunt the hare;
   Toasting, singing, jesting, laughing,
   Drive away the demon care!

HELA'R 'SGYFARNOG

1. Awn i hela'r 'sgyfarnog.
   Dyma foreu hyfryd iach;
   Codwyd hi ar graig eithinog:
   Hei! y cwn a'r gwta fach!
   Fel y gwynt, neu'n gynt na hyny,
   Gyda'r cwn a hithau'r awn;
   Ar y ffridd wrth fyn'd i fyny,
   Dyna iddi drofa iawn.

2. Am ei bywyd mae hi'n rhedeg,
   Efo'r clawdd a godrau'r llwyn:
   Wele filgi fel yn heded,
   Dyna hi o flaen ei drwyn.
   Hir y byddo mewn cadraeth,
   Hela gyda gwledd a shan:
   O! am ddysgu Naw Helwriaeth,
   Camp au gweldig Cymru lan!

1. Over hill and plain they're bounding,
   Thro' the air they seem to fly,
   Hark! the merry horn is sounding,
   List! the hunter's jovial cry!
   Now thro' dingle, dell and hollow,
   Dart they on at fearless pace;
   Oh! what joy the hounds to follow,
   There's no pleasure like the chase.

2. When the day's glad sport is over,
   Seated in the Baron's hall,
   Round the festive board discover
   Gallant hunters one and all,
   Laughing loudly, joking, singing,
   As the wine goes round apace,
   While the ancient roof is ringing
   With the glories of the chase!

from: *Songs of Wales,* by Ceirog Hughes and
Brinley Richards, Boosey & Co., 1873.

This song is to be found in most collections of Welsh melodies. Its excitement is captured in the lively setting by Haydn, with the octave leaps of the melody reflected in the octaves in contrary motion in the bass. Charles H. Purday gives the following legend relating to the song in *The Songs of Wales* by Purday and Thomas (1874):

The Church of Pennant, about two miles from Llangynog, is famed for being the burial-place of St. Monacella, reputed to have been the patroness of the hares. Monacella, who was the daughter of an Irish prince whom she displeased by refusing to marry a nobleman he had selected for her, vowing celibacy she fled her country and sought refuge in North Wales, where she lived in seclusion for fifteen years. It chanced, however, that Brochwel Ysthrog, Prince of Powis, pursued a hare into her retreat, which took refuge beneath her robe while she was engaged in her devotion, boldly defying the dogs who, fearing to approach the saint, stood howling at a distance. Brochwel, impressed alike with the beauty and sanctity of St. Monacella, and being acquainted with her history, founded an abbey and richly endowed it with lands, giving the rule of it to Monacella, who made it a sanctuary for the perfect security of all who should repair thither for safety. Monacella lived to a good old age and was extensively revered for her saintly virtues. Through her district, for a long period, hares were called "Monacella's lambs." And until the 17th century no person would put a hare to death in that district. And even at a much later period, it was firmly believed that if anyone seeing a hare pursued by dogs would cry, "God and Monacella be with you",—it would certainly escape. This legend is perpetuated in the said church by some sculptures representing hares running for protection to the saint.

35

MEN OF HARLECH

JOSEF HAYDN (1732–1809)

Maestoso con molto spirito

1. Daunt - less sons of Cel — tic sires Whose souls the love of
1. Hen - ffych well i wlad fy ngha - lon, Llwydd - iant i ti
   Per - aidd yw dy hy - nod ha - nes, I wres - og - i

free - dom fires, Hark! ev - 'ry harp to war in - spires On
Cym - ru dir - ion; Ben - dith i dy fei - ion dew - rion,
serch fy myn - wes; Tra bo 'ngwaed yn llif - o'n gy - nes,

MUSIC AND ENGLISH TEXT SOURCE: G. Thomson.

Ca - der Id - ris side. See the brave ad -
A dy ferch - ed glan; An - wyl wlad fy
Car - af wlad y gan. Hir - aeth sydd i'm

vanc - ing, See the brave ad - vanc - ing, Each
nhad - au, Car - af dy fyn - ydd - au;
lleth - u, Am an - wyl - ion Cym - ru,

well - tried spear Which Sax - ons fear, In war - like spen - dour
Craig - iau glis - ion uwch - y nant Ym - wel - ant a'r cy -
Ow! na chawn fy mhwrs yn llawn, A chred a dawn i'm

glanc - ing. Proud Har - lech from her frown - ing tow'rs Pours
myl - au, Dol - ydd a dy - ffryn - oedd ffrwth - lon,
den - u, Ad - re'n ol i blith fy nheu - lu,

forth her__ nev-er fail-ing pow'rs. Rouse, he - roes, glo - ry
Ffryd - iau__ clir a llyn - au llawn - ion, Ad - lew - yr - chant
A chy - feill - ion i'm croes - aw - u: Yn ol - yn - awl

shall be ours, March on, your coun - try's pride!
Flo - dau tlys - ion Yn ei dyffr - oedd glân:
gwnawn fol - ian - u Cym - ru, gwlad y gan.

1. Dauntless sons of Celtic sires
   Whose souls the love of freedom fires,
   Hark! ev'ry harp to war inspires
   On Cader Idris side.
   See the brave advancing,
   See the brave advancing,
   Each well-tried spear
   Which Saxons fear,
   In warlike splendour glancing.
   Proud Harlech from her frowning tow'rs
   Pours forth her never failing pow'rs.
   Rouse, heroes, glory shall be ours,
   March on, your country's pride!

2. Shall heart-rending sound of woe
   Be heard where Conway's waters flow?
   Or shall a rude and ruthless foe
   Find here one willing slave?
   From mountain and from valley,
   From mountain and from valley,
   From Snowdon, from Plinlimmon's brow
   Around your prince ye rally.
   Let cowards kiss th'oppressor's scourge,
   Home to his heart your weapons urge,
   O'erwhelm him in th'avenging surge;
   To victory, ye brave!

WELSH TEXT BY TALHAIARN

1. Henffych well, i wlad fy nghalon,
   Llwyddiant i ti Cymru dirion;
   Bendith i dy feiion dewrion,
   A dy ferched glan;
   Peraidd yw dy hynod hanes,
   I wresogi serch fy mynwes;
   Tra bo 'ngwaed yn llifo'n gynes,
   Caraf wlad y gan.

   Anwyl wlad fy nhadau,
   Caraf dy fynyddau;
   Creigiau gleision uwchy nant
   Ymwelant a'r cymylau,
   Dolydd a dyffrynoedd ffrwythlon,
   Ffrydiau clir a llynau llawnion,
   Adlewyrchant Flodau tlysion
   Yn ei dyffroedd glan:

Hiraeth sydd i'm llethu,
Am anwylion Cymru,
Ow! na chawn fy mhwrs yn llawn,
A chred a dawn i'm denu,
Adre'n ol i blith fy nheulu,
A chyfeillion i'm croesawu:
Yn olynawl gwnawn folianu
Cymru, gwlad y gan.

2. Mil melusach i fy nghalon,
   Na mwynderau gwlad y Saeson,
   Cig a gwin, a da digon,
   Ydyw gwlad y gan:
   Nid oes modd i 'ngwen lawenu,
   Tra bo 'fenaid yn hiraethu
   Am fynyddoedd cribog Cymru,
   A'i dyffrynoedd glan;

   Nid y llawn heolydd,
   Mwg a thwrf y trefydd;
   Nid y byd a'i olud drud,
   Sy'n denu bryd y prydydd;
   Ond afonydd, gwyrddion ddolydd,
   Swn yr awel yn y coedydd,
   Cymau, glynau, bryniau bronydd,
   Cymru, gwlad y gan.

   Cara'r oen y ddafad,
   Cara mun ei chariad,
   Cara'r cybydd bwrs yn llawn,
   A dyn a dawn ei dyniad;
   Cara'r babi fron ei fami,
   Caraf finau'r wlad wy'n foli,
   Duw a wyr mor anwyl i mi
   Ydyw Cymru lan.

Harlech is a town in Merionethshire, Wales, seashore site of the ruins of a celebrated fortress. Its name is derived from its location—"above the boulders," or "ar-lech" in Welsh. The fortress, believed to have originally been built by Prince Gwynedd in A.D. 530, was rebuilt by Edward I in 1282. In the fifteenth century, King Edward IV of England sent an army to take the castle from the Welsh. A siege resulting in famine forced the capitulation by the defenders.

The repeat marks are indicated in the music to accommodate the Welsh lyrics. Cymru (pronounced "Koemrie") is the Welsh name for Wales, where this song is equivalent to a national anthem.

36

SIR WATKYN'S DREAM

(Llwyn Onn)

(The Ash Grove)

ANNE HUNTER (C. 1800)　　　　　　　　　JOSEF HAYDN (1732–1809)

Allegretto

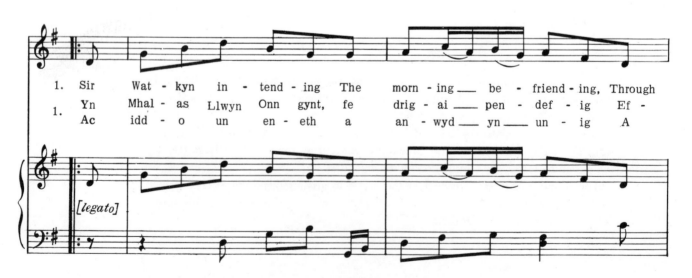

1. Sir Wat - kyn in - tend - ing The morn - ing __ be - friend - ing, Through

1. Yn Mhal - as Llwyn Onn gynt, fe drig - ai __ pen - def - ig Ef -

Ac idd - o un en - eth a an - wyd __ yn __ un - ig A

[legato]

MUSIC AND ENGLISH TEXT SOURCE: G. Thomson.

round him___ he___ ral - lies A train like a peer.
er - gyd___ yn___ wyr - gam i fyn - wes ei ferch.

1. Sir Watkyn intending
   The morning befriending,
   Through woodlands descending,
           To hunt the wild deer,
   Now slumb'ring, of course, sir,
   Dreams of his bay horse, sir,
   And proud of his force, sir,
           Begins his career.
   And forth as he sallies,
   Up hills and down valleys,
   Around him he rallies
           A train like a peer.

2. His hunter goes featly,
   His stag-hounds run fleetly,
   The bugle sounds sweetly,
           They raise a fat doe.
   Now turning and winding,
   Then losing, then finding,
   No obstacle minding,
           Still forward they go.
   All danger subduing,
   Impatient pursuing,
   With ardour renewing,
           Yet ever too slow.

3. Deep woods lay before them,
   Now soon closing o'er them,
   The knight to explore them,
           Dismounting moves on.
   There found the doe lying,
   Bemoaning and crying,
   As if she were dying,
           Behind a grey stone.
   When stopping to raise her,
   Before the dogs seize her,
   As brisk as a bee, sir,
           Away she was gone!

4. With whoop and with hollo,
   His merry men follow,
   She skims like a swallow,
           And flies like the wind.
   Sir Watkyn, however,
   Who quits the chase never,
   Swam over a river,
           And left them behind.

The day was fast closing,
His way he was losing,
The road was so 'posing,
    No path could he find.

5. A castle high frowning,
The lofty rock crowning,
Dim twighlight embrowning,
    Hung over his head.
And thitherward bending,
With steps slow ascending,
The courser attending,
    He cautiously led.
Now darkness o'ertaking,
And crags there was breaking,
He fell, —and awaking,
    The vision was fled!

LLWYN ONN (*The Ash Grove*)

1. *Yn Mhalas Llwyn Onn gynt,*
   fe drigai pendefig
E fe oedd ysgweiar ac
   ac ar glwydd y wlad;
Ac iddo un eneth
   a anwyd yn unig
A hi' nol yr hanes
   oedd aeres ei thad.
Aeth Cariad i'w gweled,
   yn lan a phur lencyn,
Ond codai'r ysgweiar
   yn afar ac erch,
I saeth-u'r bachgenyn,
   ond gwyrodd ei— linyn,
A'i ergyd yn wyrgam
   i fynwes ei ferch.

2. *Rhy hwyr ydoedd galw*
   y saeth at y llwyn
A'r llances yn marw yn welw
   yn welw a gwan;
Bygythiodd ei gleddyf
   trwy galon y llencyn;
Ond ni redai Cariad
   un fodfedd o'r fan.
'Roedd Golud, ei "despar"
   yn hen ac anynad,

1. The ash grove how graceful,
   how plainly 'tis speaking,
The harp thro' it playing
   has language for me;
Whenever the light
   thro' its branches is breaking,
A host of kind faces
   is gazing at me.
The friends of my childhood
   again are before me,
Each step wakes a mem'ry,
   as freely I roam,
With soft whispers laden,
   its leaves rustle o'er me,
The ash grove, the ash grove
   alone is my home.

2. My lips smile no more,
   my heart loses its lightness,
No dream of the future
   my spirit can cheer;
I only would brood
   on the past and its brightness,
The dead I have mourned
   are again living here.
From ev'ry dark nook
   they press forward to meet me,

A geiriau diweddaf	I lift up my eyes
yr Aeres hardd hon,	to the broad leafy dome,
Oedd, "gwell genyf farw	And others are there
trwy Ergyd fy Nghariad,	looking downward to greet me,
Na byw gyda Golud	The ash grove, the ash grove
yn Mhalas Llwyn On."	alone is my home.

from: *One Hundred Folksongs of All Nations* edited by Granville Bantock, Oliver Ditson Co. 1911, English text by John Oxenford

Llwyn Onn was the name of a mansion near Wrexham that was owned by a Mr. Jones. There is very little information to be found about this song despite its great popularity. The only other point that is discussed by William Chappell is that the tune is the same as the English "Cease Your Funning." Chappell claims its priority for the English. However, it is generally accepted as Welsh.

The tune is basically a simple triadic melody, and therefore most suitable for the harp, the national instrument of Wales. Over the years, the melody has been ornamented in many ways. Two versions are cited below for comparison with Haydn's setting and as illustration of variation due to the process of folksong evolution.

Johann Christian Bach (1735–1782), the "London Bach," includes this tune as one of the themes in the Rondo movement of his Sonata in F Major for piano duet.

Haydn has made this arrangement "con amore," skillfully suggesting imitations and turning his phrases in his best chamber music manner.

37

THE LIVE LONG NIGHT

(*Ar Hyd Nos*)

JOSEF HAYDN (1732–1809)

What a - vails thy plain - tive cry - ing, Hush, ____ ba - by, hush,
Holl am - rant - au'r ser ddy - wed - ant, Ar ____ hyd y nos,

Though a corpse thy fa ____ ther's ly - ing,
"Dym - a'r ffordd i fro ____ go - go - niant,"

MUSIC AND ENGLISH TEXT SOURCE: G. Thomson.

1. What avails thy plaintive crying,
   Hush, baby, hush,
   Though a corpse thy father's lying,
   Hush, baby, hush.
   Tears and sobs in vain endeavor
   Back to call the mourn'd forever,
   Never wilt thou see him, never,
   Hush, baby, hush.

2. See! my grief no tears are telling,
   Hush, baby, hush,
   Hark! my breast no sighs are swelling,
   Hush, baby, hush.
   No complaint or murmur making,
   Nought betrays my heart is aching,
   Yet it's breaking, sweet one, breaking,
   Hush, baby, hush.

3. Did the light'ning's flash alarm you?
   Hush, baby, hush.
   While I hold you nought shall harm you,
   Hush, baby, hush.
   Close, and closer, still I press thee,
   Soothe thee still and still caress thee,
   See! he smiles! Oh! bless thee, bless thee!
   Hush, baby, hush!

AR HYD NOS

TRANSLATION BY WALTER MAYNARD:

1. Holl amrantau'r ser ddywedant,
   Ar hyd y nos,
   "Dyma'r ffordd i fro gogoniant,"
   Ar hyd y nos.
   Golen arall yw tywyllwch,
   I arddaug os gwir brydferthwch,
   Teulur nef oedd mewn tawelwch,
   Ar hyd y nos.

2. O mor siriol gwena seren,
   Ar hyd y nos,
   I oleno'i chwaerddaearen,
   Ar hyd y nos.
   Nos yw henaint pan ddaw cystudd,
   Ond i harddu dyn a'i hwyrddyd,
   Rho'wn ein golen gwan i'n gilydd,
   Ar hyd y nos.

1. Love, fear not if sad thy dreaming
   All thro' the night,
   Though o'ercast, bright stars are gleaming
   All thro' the night.
   Joy will come to thee at morning,
   Life with sunny hope adorning,
   Though sad dreams may give dark warning
   All thro' the night.

2. Angels watching ever round thee
   All thro' the night,
   In thy slumbers close surround thee
   All thro' the night.
   They should of all fear disarm thee,
   No forebodings should alarm thee,
   They will let no peril harm thee,
   All thro' the night.

1. Look at me, my little dear,
      Un, dau, tri,
   Let me whisper in thine ear,
      Un, dau, tri;
   Bid thy playmates all retire,
      Sit thee down and draw thee nigher,
      See the bright inviting fire,
      Un, dau, tri.

2. Softly fall the shades of night
      Un, dau, tri,
   Lady moon is shining bright,
      Un, dau, tri;
   In a bed of yellow gold,
   I my little lamb will fold,
   Safely hid from winter cold,
      Un, dau, tri.

from: Alfred Moffat, *Minstrelsy of Wales,* 1906

Generally known as "All Through the Night," this lullaby is widely popular beyond the shores of Wales. There are several other texts to the tune, of which one of the better known was by Mrs. Opie: "There beneath a willow sleepeth Poor Mary Anne."

John Parry, the blind bard of the eighteenth century known as Bardd Alaw, gave the following note on the song: "Cwsg was the Somnus of ancient Britain; he used to send his priest Einion Lonydd (Einion the Soother) to put the children to sleep."

38

MERCH MEGAN; OR PEGGY'S DAUGHTER

ANNE HUNTER (C. 1800)

LUDWIG VAN BEETHOVEN (1770–1827)

1. In the white cot where Peg - gy dwells, — Her daugh - ter fair the rose — ex - cells That round her case - ment sweet - ly blows, — And
A wels - och chwi 'riodd mo E - lin, merch Me - gan, O gwm - pas ei gwaith yn ddi - wyd a llon? Bydd cys - ur - a mwyn - iant o'i gwyn - eb yn — t'wyn - u Wrth
Mae pob - peth a wnel yn bles - er i'w wel - ed, A'i gwen yn y ty fel heul - wen ar don;

MUSIC AND ENGLISH TEXT SOURCE: G. Thomson, also *Beethoven's Werke,* Breitkopf and Härtel.

on _____ the gale _____ its fra - grance throws. ___ O were she mine, the
ol - chi a smwdd - io a gweith - io'n ddi - gwyn; Yn ber - aidd o'i min bydd

love - ly maid! ___ She soon ___ would leave the lone - ly shade.
miw - sig yn llif - o, Mor swyn - ol a llais yr E - os mewn llwyn.

sfp

cresc.

1. In the white cot where Peggy dwells,
   Her daughter fair the rose excells
   That round her casement sweetly blows,
   And on the gale its fragrance throws.
   O were she mine, the lovely maid!
   She soon would leave the lonely shade.

2. I'd bear her where the beams of morn
   Should with their brightest rays adorn
   Each budding charm and op'ning grace,
   That moulds her form and decks her face.
   O were she mine, the lovely maid!
   I'd bear her from the lonely shade.

3. But, should the sultry orb of day
   Too fiercely dart his fervid ray,
   The rose upon its stalk might die,
   And zephir o'er its ruins sight!
   No— I would keep my lovely maid
   Secure beneath the friendly shade.

MERCH MEGAN

WELSH AND ENGLISH TEXT BY TALHAIARN

1. { A welsoch chwi 'riodd mo Elin, merch Megan,
   { O gwmpas ei gwaith yn ddiwyd a llon?
   { Mae pobpeth a wnel yn bleser i'w weled,
   { A'i gwen yn y ty fel heulwen ar don;
     Bydd cysura mwyniant o'i gwyneb yn t'wynu
     Wrth olchi a smwddio a gweithio'n ddigwyn;
     Yn beraidd o'i min bydd miwsig yn llifo,
     Mor swynol a llais yr Eos mewn llwyn.

2. { Mae Elin yn lan a gonest ei chalon,
   { Ei phurdeb a'i ffydd yn glodus drwy'n gwlad:
   { Caredig yw hi, a hoffus a thirion,
   { Anwylyd ei mam,— llaweydd ei thad:
     Flynonell cysuron a thelyn anwyliant
     Fydd Elin f'anwylyd pan unir nyni:
     Wrth deithio drwy'r byd mewn hedd a boddlondeb,
     Dedwyddyd fydd hi bob munyd i mi.

1. { Oh, have you e'er seen the daughter of Megan,
   { So gentle and kind, so tender and true?
   { She's bright as the wave that curls on the ocean,
   { And sweet as the rose when glist'ning with dew;
     Her smile is bewitching, her movements are charming,
     While busily working to keep the house clean;
     The sunshine of joy enhances her beauty,
     And innocent love glows in her sweet mein.

2. { How dear to my heart is Megan's fair daughter,
   { Grace, virtue, and faith have hallow'd her life:
   { A maid who is good and kind to her mother
   { Will always be kind and true as a wife:
     When we are united together in wedlock,
     The daughter of Megan a blessing will prove,
     While labour with health and peace with contentment
     Will make our sweet home a dwelling of love.

from: *Gems of Welsh Melody*
arranged by John Owen (Owain Alaw) Wrexham: Hughes & Son

The song is variously known as "Megan's Daughter," "Peggy's Daughter," and "Margaret's Daughter." This graceful melody has been set by Beethoven to an equally lovely undulating accompaniment, reminiscent of some of his lieder or of the rondo movement of his Piano Sonata Op. 90. Beethoven also composed a set of variations on this tune, called erroneously *Air Ecossais,* no. 6 in *Ten Varied Themes for Piano Alone, or with Flute or Violin,* op. 107.

39

WAKEN, LORDS AND LADIES GAY

SIR WALTER SCOTT (1771–1832) LUDWIG VAN BEETHOVEN (1770–1827)

Allegro spiritoso

Wak - en, lords and la - dies gay, Up -
Wak - en, lords and la - dies gay, The

on the moun - tain dawns the day;
mist has left the moun - tain grey;

All the jol - ly chase is here, With
Brakes are deck'd with dia - monds bright, And

MUSIC AND TEXT SOURCE: G. Thomson, also *Beethoven's Werke*, Breitkopf and Härtel.

wak - en, lords ___ and ___ la - dies gay!
wak - en, lords ___ and ___ la - dies gay!

1. Waken, lords and ladies gay,
   Upon the mountain dawns the day;
   All the jolly chase is here
   With hawk and horse and hunting spear.
   The eager hounds in chorus cry,
   The swelling hours salute the sky;
   And merrily, merrily mingle they;
   Then waken, lords and ladies gay!

2. Waken, lords and ladies gay,
   The mist has left the mountain grey;
   Brakes are deck'd with diamonds bright,
   And streams rejoice in early light.
   The foresters have busy been
   To track the buck in thicket green;
   Now we are come to chaunt our lay;
   Then waken, lords and ladies gay!

3. Waken, lords and ladies gay,
   Unto the green wood haste away;
   We can shew you where he lies,
   Fleet of foot and tall of size:
   And we can shew the marks he made,
   When 'gainst the oak his antlers fray'd;
   You soon shall see him brought to bay;
   Then waken, lords and ladies gay!

4. Louder, louder, chaunt the lay,
   O waken, lords and ladies gay;
   Tell them, Youth and Mirth and Glee,
   Run swift their course as well as we:
   Old Time, stern huntsman! who can baulk,
   As staunch as hound and fleet as hawk;
   O think of this and rise with day,
   Ye gentle lords and ladies gay!

In this exciting setting by Beethoven, one can almost hear the hunting horns, the baying hounds, and the sound of galloping horses.

Under the title of "Conset y siri" or "Sheriff's Delight," or "Sheriff's Fancy," this, like other well-known tunes, was a basic theme for pennillion singing. Pennillion is an old Welsh form of improvised vocal variations in rhyme over a melody that is carried in the harp accompaniment. The art is cultivated within a framework of strict rules, and contests of pennillion singers have flourished in Wales for centuries. The tune is given here as it was played at an "Eisteddfod," or singing contest, in the town of Battlesden in 1862:

from: *Gems of Welsh Melody* by John Owen, (1873)

V

AMERICAN SONGS

Although folk songs had been transplanted in the United States from European and African stock, they have taken root and borne some distinctive, hybrid fruits. From the Anglo-Celtic branch there developed the ballads of the hill folk and "bluegrass" music, the cowboy songs, the white spirituals, and square dances. From the Negro came the minstrel tunes, the spirituals, work songs, cakewalks, blues, ragtime, and jazz. There was much overlapping and borrowings between them, and there were other later influences from Europe and Latin America. What has emerged is a native folk culture that reflects life in a new land—a varied and vigorous folk music.

American composers have been ambivalent in their attitude toward our folk song. On the one hand, shunning it, they rather emulated the abstract forms of the great European composers. But at the same time many were intrigued by our folk and popular music and sought a national idiom. George Gershwin found in the blues and jazz the embodiment of folk expression and composed works that are regarded as truly American. Unfortunately, because permission to reprint was not granted, his "Street Cries" from *Porgy and Bess* could not be included in this book. Other composers, among whom are Gottschalk, Ives, Thomson, Harris, Cowell, and Copland, have based some of their serious works on American folk material.

40

THE BANJO

('Twill Never Do to Give It up So) (Camptown Races)

LOUIS MOREAU GOTTSCHALK (1829–1869)

1. I'm ol' Mis-ter Brown, just from the South, I left Lynch-burg in the
   Ol' Jim riv-er I float-ed down, My back-er boat it

   time of the drought; The times they got so bad in the place That the
   run upon the groun'; The pine log came with a rush-in' din And

MUSIC SOURCE: *The Banjo,* Willum Hall & Son, New York, 1855. Music abridged.
Vocal line and text added by editor.

CHORUS

black folks dare not show their face. 'Twill nev-er do to give it up
stove both ends of the ol' boat in.

so, 'Twill nev-er do to give it up so, 'Twill nev-er do to give it up

so, Mis-ter Brown, 'Twill nev-er do to give it up so.

bob - tail nag, Some - bod - y bet on the bay. 2. The

ben misurato, animato

long - tail fil - ly and the big black hoss,
blind hoss stick - in' in a big black mud hole,

un poco più f, martellato [sempre cresc. poco a poco]

Doo - dah! doo - dah! They fly the track and they
Doo - dah! doo - dah! Can't touch bot - tom with a

both cut a - cross, Doo - dah, doo - dah day! The
ten foot pole, Doo - dah, doo - dah day!

CHORUS

Goin' to run all night, Goin' to run all

[accel. e cresc. al fine]

day, I'll bet my mon-ey on the bob-tail nag,

D. S.

Some-bod-y bet on the bay. 3. Ol'

[cresc.]

fff

1. I'm ol' Mister Brown, just from the South,
   I left Lynchburg in the time of the drought;
   The times they got so bad in the place
   That the black folks dare not show their face.

CHORUS: 'Twill never do to give it up so,
   'Twill never do to give it up so,
   'Twill never do to give it up so, Mister Brown,
   'Twill never do to give it up so.

2. Ol' Jim River I floated down,
   My backer boat it run upon the groun';
   The pine log came with a rushin' din
   And stove both ends of the ol' boat in. *Chorus:*

3. Ol' log rake me aft and fore,
   It left my cook-house on the shore;
   I thought it wouldn't do to give it up so,
   So I scull myself ashore with the ol' banjo. *Chorus:*

4. Master on the woodpile barkin' like a dog,
   Toad in the millpond settin' on a log;
   Possum up a gum tree, saucy, fat, and dirty,
   Come kiss me gals or I'll run like a turkey. *Chorus:*

CAMPTOWN RACES

STEPHEN FOSTER
(1826–1864)

1. Camptown ladies sing this song,
   Doodah! doodah!
   Camptown racetrack five miles long,
   Doodah, doodah day!
   Come down there with my hat caved in,
   Doodah! doodah!
   I go back home with a pocket full of tin,
   Doodah, doodah day!

CHORUS: Goin' to run all night,
   Goin' to run all day,
   I'll bet my money on the bobtail nag,
   Somebody bet on the bay.

2. The long-tail filly and the big black hoss,
     Doodah! doodah!
   They fly the track and they both cut across,
     Doodah, doodah day!
   The blind hoss stickin' in a big mud hole,
     Doodah! doodah!
   Can't touch bottom with a ten foot pole,
     Doodah, doodah day! *Chorus:*

3. Ol' muley cow come onto the track,
     Doodah! doodah!
   The bobtail fling her over his back,
     Doodah, doodah day!
   Then fly along like a railroad car,
     Doodah! doodah!
   Runnin' a race with a shootin' star,
     Doodah, doodah day! *Chorus:*

4. See them flyin' on a ten-mile heat,
     Doodah! doodah!
   'Round the race track, then repeat,
     Doodah, doodah day!
   I win my money on the bobtail nag,
     Doodah! doodah!
   I keep my money in an ol' towbag,
     Doodah, doodah day! *Chorus:*

'Twill Never Do to Give It up So

The printed sheet music of this song (1843) carries the subtitle "A Favorite Banjo Song" and claims the authorship of Dan Emmett of the Ethiopian Serenaders. However, many Negro songs were adapted by popular songwriters and burnt-cork performers, and such may well have been the case with this tune. Gottschalk, whose mother was Creole, was totally opposed to the minstrel show. He may have derived his tune from a common source, or he may have heard and liked the tune, unaware of its minstrel origin. There is a version in Norman Cazden's *A Book of Nonsense Songs,* recently published, where the song is named "The Gollycully."

Camptown Races

The Negro spiritual "Roll Jordan, Roll" seems to have been the basic melody from which Stephen Foster's "Camptown Races" stemmed and which also serves for Gottschalk's "The Banjo." As a piano piece, "The Banjo," Op. 15, is an integration of American folk music into concert form. It was composed by Gottschalk as a virtuoso vehicle for his programs. He was a world-renowned pianist and was especially acclaimed in the Western Hemisphere. Many of his distinctive works are based on American and Latin American folk music.

41

WADE IN THE WATER

SAMUEL COLERIDGE-TAYLOR (1875–1912)

Wade _____ in the wa - ter, Wade _____ in the

MUSIC SOURCE: *Twenty-Four Negro Melodies,* transcribed by Samuel Coleridge-Taylor, Oliver
Ditson Co., 1905. Music abridged.
Vocal line and text added by the editor.

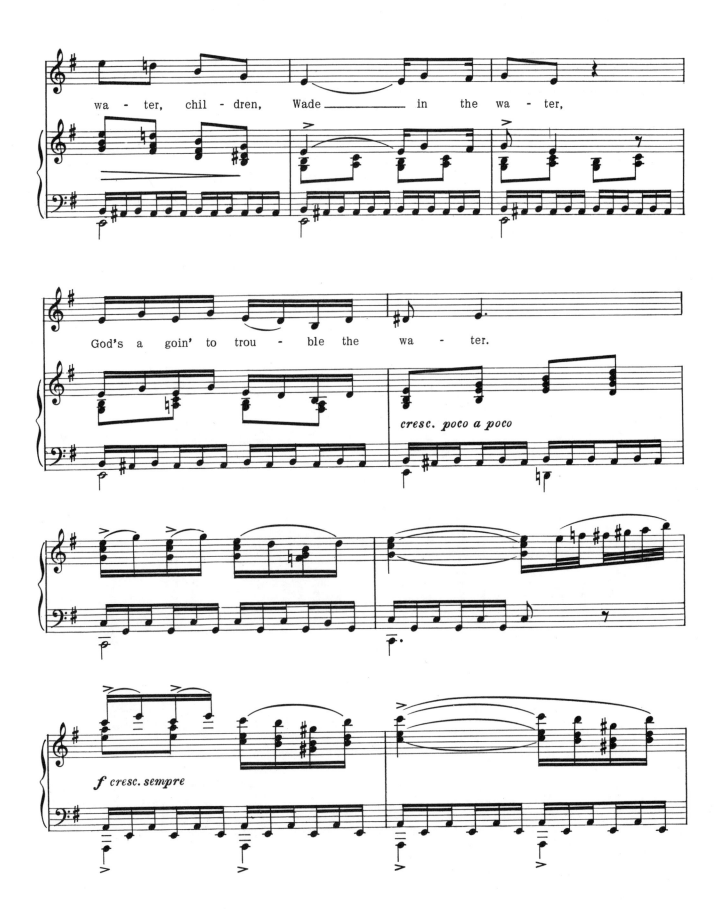

wa - ter, chil - dren, Wade _____ in the wa - ter,

God's a goin' to trou - ble the wa - ter.

cresc. poco a poco

f cresc. sempre

1. Wade in the water,
   Wade in the water, children,
   Wade in the water,
   God's a goin' to trouble the water.

2. Wade in the water,
   Wade in the water, children,
   Wade in the water,
   Wade in the water and be baptized.

The music of black Americans has been a stimulus to many famous composers from Dvořák to Stravinsky. It is natural that it should also be a source of inspiration to Negro composers. Many works of Samuel Coleridge-Taylor, the English composer, reflect the consciousness of his racial heritage. In his preface to *Twenty-Four Negro Melodies* (1904), the composer states: "What Brahms has done for the Hungarian folk music, Dvořák for the Bohemian, and Grieg for the Norwegian, I have tried to do for these Negro Melodies." These were written for the piano as instrumental elaborations, mostly in the form of theme with a few variations interspersed with modulating episodic passages. They bear the earmarks of the late Victorian period when they were written. The song text is presented here with an abridged version of the piano setting.

Many of the spirituals during slavery, prior to the Civil War, had double meanings, clandestine messages to aid in escaping to the North. Such phrases as "wade in the water," "steal away to Jesus," and "Michael, row the boat ashore" really gave direction for the slaves to the underground railroad and freedom.

42

A SON OF A GAMBOLIER

CHARLES IVES (1874–1954)

In a fast two-step time

1.

2.

1. Come join my hum-ble dit-ty, ____ From Tip-per-y town I steer, ____ Like
2. (I) wish I had a bar-rel of rum, and su-gar three hun-dred pound, ____ The

ev - ery hon - est fel - low, ____ I take my la - ger beer; Like
col - lege bell to mix it in, the clap-per to stir it round; I'd

ev - ery hon - est fel - low, ____ I take my whis - key clear. I'm a
drink the health of dear old Yale and friends both far and near.

ram - bling rake of pov - er - ty and a son of a gam - bo - lier. 2. I   lier.

1. Come join my humble ditty, from Tippery town I steer,
   Like every honest fellow, I take my lager beer;
   Like every honest fellow, I take my whiskey clear.
   I'm a rambling rake of poverty and a son of a gambolier.

2. I wish I had a barrel of rum, and sugar three hundred pound,
   The college bell to mix it in, the clapper to stir it round;
   I'd drink the health of dear old Yale and friends both far and near.
   I'm a rambling rake of poverty and a son of a gambolier.

additional verses, not in the Ives song:

3. In the town of Ithica I've often cut a dash,
   I've learned the secret long ago to use my cheek for cash;
   I'm in with all the pretty girls, who call me "little dear,"
   For I'm a rambling rake of poverty and a son of a gambolier.

4. O, many a jolly time I've had, all through my college life,
   And when my sheepskin I obtain, I'll look then for a wife;
   I'll ask some girl that's got the rocks to wed me else I'll die,
   For I'm a rambling rake of poverty and a son of a gambolier.

5. She'll answer me in tones so sweet, "Yes, love, I will be thine,"
   And with the governor's pocketbook, O won't we cut a shine;
   We'll drive out in the park each day, O how is that for high,
   For I'm a rambling rake of poverty and a son of a gambolier.

TEXT SOURCE FOR ADDITIONAL VERSES: *Carmina Collegensia,* Oliver Ditson Co., 1876.

This song has been adopted by several colleges, among them Yale and Cornell, but it is most famous as "I'm a Rambling Wreck from Georgia Tech." Charles Ives made this setting in 1895 as one of a group of "Five Street Pieces."

The piano part is quite full; it is rather like a condensed score for a band arrangement. In fact, it has all the tongue-in-cheek clichés of band scoring, even to the point of naming the instrumental voicings. The early trademark of Ives is evident— a distinct feeling of Americana, which is here and there manifest through a rakish syncopation, a blues harmony, use of a declassed instrument like the kazoo, and an irrelevant and irreverent quotation. (Mendelssohn's "Wedding March" appears on the scene just before the final chorus!) The extra verses can be adapted to be sung during the kazoo chorus. There are also additional verses in Carl Sandburg's *American Songbag* (1927).

43

MY SHEPHERD WILL SUPPLY MY NEED

ISAAC WATTS (1674–1748)　　　　　　　　　　VIRGIL THOMSON (1896–　　)

Allegro ma sostenuto

My Shep - herd will sup - ply my need, Je - ho - vah is his Name. In pas - tures fresh he makes me feed Be - side the liv - ing stream. He

1. My Shepherd will supply my need,   7.5
   Jehovah *is* his Name.
   In pastures fresh he makes me feed
   Beside the living stream.
   He brings my wand'ring spirit back
   When I forsake his ways.
   He leads me for his mercy's sake
   In paths of truth and grace.

2. When I walk through the shades of death
   Thy presence *is* my stay.
   One word of thy supporting breath
   Drives all my fears away.
   Thy hand, in sight of all my foes
   Doth still my table spread.
   My cup with blessings overflows,
   Thine oil anoints my head.

3. The sure provisions of my God
   Attend me all my days.
   O may thy house be my abode
   And all my work be praise.
   There would I find a settled rest,
   While others go and come.
   No more a stranger or a guest,
   But like a child at home.

This metrical version of the Twenty-Third Psalm is by the English hymn writer Isaac Watts (1674–1748). The tune, entitled "Resignation," appears with these verses in William Walker's *Southern Harmony,* 1854. It is the type of pentatonic melody found in many shaped-note hymnals still in use today in rural areas, especially in the southern Appalachian Mountains. The notes in these hymn books are placed on the customary lines and spaces of the staff, but each note of the scale has its own shape.

Do Mi   Sol   Mi Re   Do   Sol   Do   La Sol   Mi

Thus the layman, learning to sing his "do–re–mi" according to the shape of the note, joined in part singing at the religious camp-meeting or in church. Here the oral tradition merged with written music of the "singing school," and a new type of choral folk music emerged. I vividly recall how seriously and enthusiastically a congregation choir in West Virginia sang solfeggio from the hymnal. At the same time, I remember with what vigor a carpenter from that village chanted one of these hymns as he labored at his trade!

Speaking of the tune of "My Shepherd," Virgil Thomson says:

Certainly its arpeggiated structure has its origin in the sound of hunting horns. Its soaring curve, however, and its well-prepared climax suggest an Irish source of the late seventeenth or early eighteenth century. The accompaniment, though it outlines horn calls, is essentially an evocation of organ playing.

44

THE DODGER (*Campaign Song*)

AARON COPLAND (1900–)

Heavy, not too fast

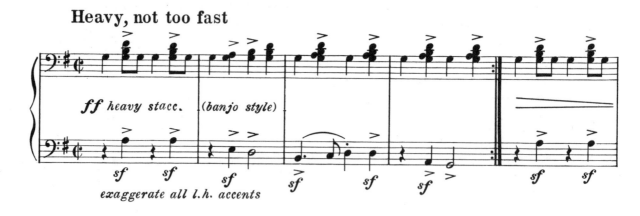

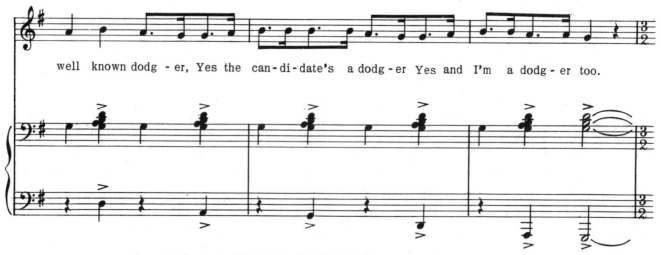

He'll meet you and treat you and ask you for your vote, But look out, boys, — he's a dodg-in' for a note. Yes we're all dodg-in'— A-dodg-in', dodg-in', dodg-in', Yes we're all dodg-in' Out a way through the world.

look out, boys,＿ He's a dodg-in' for your dimes. Yes we're all

2.

lov-er he's a dodg-er, Yes a well known dodg-er, Yes the

lov-er he's a dodg-er, Yes and I'm a dodg-er too. He'll

hug you and kiss you And call you his bride, But

1. Yes the candidate's a dodger,
   Yes a well known dodger,
   Yes the candidate's a dodger
   Yes and I'm a dodger too.
   He'll meet you and treat you
   And ask you for your vote,
   But look out, boys,
   He's a-dodgin' for a note.

CHORUS: Yes we're all dodgin'
          A-dodgin', dodgin', dodgin',
          Yes we're all dodgin'
          Out a way through the world.

2. Yes the preacher he's a dodger,
   Yes a well known dodger,
   Yes the preacher he's a dodger,
   Yes and I'm a dodger too.
   He'll preach you a gospel
   And tell you of your crimes,
   But look out, boys,
   He's a-dodgin' for your dimes.

CHORUS: Yes we're all dodgin'
          A-dodgin', dodgin', dodgin',
          Yes we're all dodgin'
          Out a way through the world.

3. Yes the lover he's a dodger,
   Yes a well known dodger,
   Yes the lover he's a dodger,
   Yes and I'm a dodger too.
   He'll hug you and kiss you
   And call you his bride,
   But look out, girls,
   He's a-tellin' you a lie.

CHORUS: Yes we're all dodgin'
          A-dodgin', dodgin', dodgin',
          Yes we're all dodgin'
          Out a way through the world.

4. Yes the lawyer he's a dodger,
   Yes a well-known dodger,
   Yes the lawyer he's a dodger,
   Yes and I'm a dodger too.
   He'll plead you a case
   And claim you as a friend,
   But look out, boys,
   He's easy for to bend! *Chorus:*

5. Yes the doctor he's a dodger,
   Yes a well known dodger,
   Yes the doctor he's a dodger,
   Yes and I'm a dodger too.
   He'll doctor you and cure you
   For half you possess,
   But look out, boys,
   He's a-dodgin' for the rest! *Chorus:*

6. Yes the merchant he's a dodger,
   Yes a well known dodger,
   Yes the merchant he's a dodger,
   Yes and I'm a dodger too.
   He'll sell you goods
   At double the price,
   But when you go to pay him,
   You'll have to pay him twice! *Chorus:*

7. Yes the farmer he's a dodger,
   Yes a well known dodger,
   Yes the farmer he's a dodger,
   Yes and I'm a dodger too.
   He'll plow his cotton,
   He'll plow his corn,
   He'll make a living
   Just as sure as you're born! *Chorus:*

The Special Skills Division of the Resettlement Administration in 1936 sent musicians to the rural areas of selected regions of the country. One of their tasks was to notate the songs of the people. A group of these songs was printed by the government. About that time, too, the ravages of the Depression were accentuated by the severe drought, and portions of Oklahoma and Arkansas became known as the "Dust Bowl." It was from this locale that Woody Guthrie emigrated singing his traditional songs and making up new ones. Among the songs collected and printed at that time was "The Dodger," as sung by Mrs. Emma Dusenberry from Mena, Arkansas. She learned it in the 1880s, when it was supposed to have been sung during the Cleveland-Blaine Presidential election campaign.

Copland has effectively embodied in his setting the banjo-style chord cluster, where the drone string of the five-string banjo sounds throughout. He has underpinned the held notes with a persistent rhythmic accompaniment that gives the phrases the right asymmetrical "primitivistic" touch. This sense of style characterizes his other works in the folk idiom, such as *Appalachian Spring* and *Billy the Kid.*

OTHER ARRANGEMENTS OF
FOLK SONGS BY
SERIOUS COMPOSERS

ENGLISH, IRISH, SCOTTISH, AND WELSH FOLK SONGS

BAX, ARNOLD
    "Green Grow the Rashes O!," Murdoch, Murdoch & Co., 1920

BENJAMIN, ARTHUR
    "Linstead Market," Boosey & Hawkes, 1947

BRITTEN, BENJAMIN
    Folk Song Arrangements, Boosey & Hawkes, 1943

EDMUNDS, JOHN
    Folk Songs, Boston Music Co., 1953

GRAINGER, PERCY
    "Willow, Willow," Schott & Co., London, 1912
    "Died for Love," Schott & Co., London, 1912

HAYDN, JOSEPH
    A Select Collection of Original Scottish Airs, Volumes III and IV, ed. by George
    Thomson, P. Preston, London, 1803–1805

HOLST, GUSTAV
    "Folk Songs from Hampshire," in *English County Folk Songs,* ed. by Cecil Sharp, Novello and Co. Ltd., 1908–1912, in 5 vols.; reprinted in 1 vol., 1961

PLEYEL, IGNAZ
    A Select Collection of Original Scottish Airs, Volumes I and II, ed. by George Thomson, P. Preston, London, 1803–1805

RESPIGHI, OTTORINO
    Scottish Songs, Universal Edition, 1925

VAUGHAN WILLIAMS, RALPH
    Eight Traditional English Carols, Stainer & Bell, Ltd., 1919
    "Folk Songs from the Eastern Counties" (collected and arranged by R. V. W.), in *English County Folk Songs,* ed. by Cecil Sharp, Novello & Co. Ltd., 1908–1912, in 5 vols.; reprinted in 1 vol., 1961
    "Folk Songs from Sussex" (collected and arranged by R. V. W.), in *English County Folk Songs,* ed. by Cecil Sharp, Novello & Co. Ltd., 1908–1912, in 5 vols.; reprinted in 1 vol., 1961

AMERICAN FOLKSONGS

BACON, ERNST
    "Along Unpaved Roads," Delkas Music Publishers, 1944
    Songs from the American Folk, Carl Fischer, Inc., 1946
    "The Erie Canal," Carl Fischer, Inc., 1942

BURLEIGH, HARRY
    Negro Spirituals, Franco Colombo, 1917–1928

CAZDEN, NORMAN
    American Folk Songs for Piano (with text), Jack Spratt Music, 1962

COLERIDGE-TAYLOR, SAMUEL
    Twenty Four Negro Melodies, Oliver Ditson, Co., 1905

COPLAND, AARON
    Old American Songs, Boosey & Hawkes, 1950–1952

DETT, NATHANIEL
    Spirituals, Mills Music, Inc., 1946

DOUGHERTY, CELIUS
    Five American Folk Songs, G. Schirmer, Inc., 1953

EDMUNDS, JOHN
    Folk Songs, Boston Music Co., 1953

HAUFRECHT, HERBERT, in collaboration with GARSON, EUGENIA
    Laura Ingalls Wilder Songbook, Harper & Row, 1968

GERSHWIN, GEORGE
    Porgy and Bess (street cries from the opera), Gershwin Publishing Corp., 1935; also Random House, 1935

GRUENBERG, LOUIS
    Negro Spirituals, Universal Editions, 1926

POWELL, JOHN
    Five Virginia Folk Songs, J. Fischer & Bro., 1938
    "Soldier, Soldier," J. Fischer & Bro., 1936
    Twelve Folk Hymns, J. Fischer & Bro., 1934

ROBINSON, EARL
    Young Folks Song Book, Simon & Schuster, Inc., 1963

SIEGMEISTER, ELIE
    Singing Down the Road, Ginn & Co., 1947
    " 'Way Up on Old Smoky," Ginn & Co., 1950
    Work and Sing, W. R. Scott, Inc., 1944

STILL, WILLIAM GRANT
    Twelve Negro Spirituals, Handy Brothers Music Co., Inc., 1937

BIBLIOGRAPHY

ENGLISH

BARRETT, WILLIAM ALEXANDER
  English Folk-Songs, Novello, Ewer and Co., London, 1891

BASKERVILL, CHARLES R.
  The Elizabethan Jig, University of Chicago Press, 1929; reprint, Dover Publications, 1965

BRONSON, BERTRAND
  The Traditional Tunes of the Child Ballads, Princeton University Press, 1959–1966

CHAPPELL, WILLIAM
  Old English Popular Music, 1893; reprint, J. Brussel, New York, 1961
  Popular Music of the Olden Time, 1855; reprint, Dover Publications, 1965

CHILD, FRANCIS J.
  The English and Scottish Popular Ballads, 1882–98; Houghton Mifflin & Co., Boston, 1904; reprint, Dover Publications, 1965

DEAN-SMITH, MARGARET
  A Guide to English Folk Song Collections, Liverpool University Press, 1954

KIDSON, FRANK, and NEAL, MARY
  English Folk Song and Dance, Cambridge at the University Press, 1915

LLOYD, A. L.
  Folksong in England, International Publishers, 1967

SHARP, CECIL
  One Hundred English Folksongs, Oliver Ditson Co., 1916
  English Folk Music, Mercury Books, 1965
SIMPSON, CLAUDE M.
  The British Broadside Ballad and Its Music, Rutgers University Press, 1966

IRISH

GALVIN, PATRICK
  Irish Songs of Resistance, Folklore Press, 1956
HUGHES, HERBERT
  Irish Country Songs, Boosey & Co., 1909
JOYCE, P. W.
  Old Irish Folk Music and Songs, Hodges, Friggis & Co., Ltd., 1909; reprint, Cooper Square Publishers, 1965
LAMPE, J. BODEWALT
  Ireland in Song, Remick Music Corp., 1916, reprint 1955
MALLOY, JAMES
  The Songs of Ireland, Boosey & Co., London, 1873
MOORE, THOMAS
  Irish Melodies, Oliver Ditson Co., 1893; also M. H. Gill and Son, Dublin, 1891
O LOCHLAINN, COLM
  Irish Street Ballads, Corinth Books, Inc., 1960
O'SULLIVAN, DONAL
  Irish Folk Music and Songs, Cultural Relations Comm. of Ireland, 1952
  Songs of the Irish, Bonanza Books, 1960
PETRIE, GEORGE
  The Complete Collection of Irish Music, Boosey & Co., 1902–1905
STANFORD, CHARLES V.
  Irish Songs and Ballads, Novello, Ewer & Co., 1893

SCOTTISH

BROWN, COLIN, and PITTMAN, JOSIAH
  The Songs of Scotland, Vol. I, Boosey & Co., 1877 (?)
COLLINSON, FRANCIS
  The Traditional and National Music of Scotland, Routledge and Kegan Paul, London, 1966
DICK, JAMES C.
  The Songs of Robert Burns, 1903; reprint, Folklore Associates, 1962
FARQUHAR-GRAHAM, GEORGE
  The Popular Songs and Melodies of Scotland, Bayley & Ferguson, 1891
JOHNSON, JAMES
  Scots Musical Museum, reprint, Folklore Associates, 2 vols., 1962
LAMPE, J. BODEWALT
  Scotland in Song, Remick Music Corp., 1914
MOFFAT, ALFRED
  The Minstrelsy of Scotland, Augener & Co., 1896
MACCOLL, EWAN
  Folk Songs and Ballads of Scotland, Oak Publications, 1965
THOMSON, WILLIAM
  Orpheus Caledonius, 1725; reprint, Folklore Associates, 1962

WELSH

MOFFAT, ALFRED
  Minstrelsy of Wales, Augener, Ltd., 1906
MOLLER, HEINRICH
  Keltische Volkslieder, B. Schotts Söhne, 1924
SOMERVELL, ARTHUR, and WILLIAMS, J. LLOYD
  Welsh Melodies, Boosey & Co., 1907

WILLIAMS, W. S. GWYNN
Welsh National Music and Dance, Curwen & Sons, London, 1932

AMERICAN

ALLEN, W. F.
Slave Songs of the U.S., 1867; reprints, Peter Smith, 1929, 1951

AMES, RUSSELL
The Story of American Folk Song, Grosset & Dunlap, 1955

BOTKIN, BENJAMIN
A Treasury of American Folklore, Crown Publishers, 1944

CAZDEN, NORMAN
The Abelard Folk Song Book, Abelard-Schuman, 1958

CHASE, GILBERT
America's Music, McGraw-Hill Book Co., 1955

DECORMIER, ROBERT, and GILBERT, RONNIE
The Weavers' Songbook, Harper and Row, 1960

DOWNES, OLIN, and SIEGMEISTER, ELIE
A Treasury of American Song, Alfred A. Knopf, 1940

HAUFRECHT, HERBERT
Folk Sing, Hollis Music, Inc., 1960
The Wayfaring Stranger, Burl Ives, Leeds Music Corp., 1945
————, and GILBERT, RONNIE
Travelin' on with the Weavers, Harper and Row, 1966

HOWARD, JOHN TASKER
Our American Music, Crowell, 4th ed., 1965

JACKSON, GEORGE PULLEN
Spiritual Folk-Songs of Early America, J. J. Augustin, 1937

JOHNSON, JAMES WELDON
The Book of American Negro Spirituals, Viking Press, 1925

KOLB, JOHN and SYLVIA
A Treasury of Folk Songs, Bantam Books, 1948

LOMAX, JOAN A. and ALAN
Best Loved American Folk Songs, Grosset & Dunlap, 1947
Folk Song U.S.A., Duell, Sloan & Pearce, 1947

SANDBERG, CARL
The American Songbag, Harcourt, Brace & Co., 1927

SCOTT, JOHN ANTHONY
The Ballad of America, Bantam Books, 1966

GENERAL

BANTOCK, GRANVILLE
One Hundred Folksongs of All Nations, Oliver Ditson Co., 1911

BOTSFORD, FLORENCE H.
Botsford Collection of Folk Songs, G. Schirmer, Inc., 1922, 1930

BONI, MARGARET B., and LLOYD, NORMAN
Fireside Book of Favorite American Songs, Simon & Schuster, Inc., 1947

BOULTON, HAROLD, and SOMERVELL, ARTHUR
Songs of the Four Nations, J. B. Cramer & Co., Ltd., 1893

GOSS, JOHN
Ballads of Britain, The Bodley Head, 1937

HAUFRECHT, HERBERT
'Round the World Folk Sing, Hollis Music Inc., 1963
Folk Songs and Ballads, Remick Music Corp., 1958

HULLAH, JOHN
The Song Book, Macmillan & Co., 1892

STANFORD, CHARLES V., and SHAW, GEOFFREY
The New National Song Book, Boosey & Co., 1906, 1938

DISCOGRAPHY

Composition	Composer	Artist	Record Label
"Fortune My Foe"	SWEELINCK	E. Power Biggs	Col. ML5737; MLS6337
"Go from My Window"	MORLEY	V. Aveling	DGG 3209; 73209
"Sellinger's Round"	BYRD	E. Bodky	* Decca DX106
"Harvest Home" (from *King Arthur*)	PURCELL	Alan	Ois. 50176/7; 60008/9
"Sally In Our Alley"	BEETHOVEN	H. Traubel	* Col. ML2085
"Salisbury Plain"	VAUGHAN WILLIAMS	A. L. Lloyd	Folk-Lyric FL121
"The Foggy Foggy Dew"	BRITTEN	P. Pears	**Decca (Eng.) CCP 711
		T. Dart	Argo (Eng) RG82/3
"Lilliburlero"	PURCELL	Guiness Choir	Cor. 57490; 757490
"Oh Who My Dearest Dermot"	BEETHOVEN	R. Dyer-Bennet	DYB 7000
"The Pulse of An Irishman"	BEETHOVEN	R. Dyer-Bennet	DYB 7000
"The Soldier"	BEETHOVEN	H. Traubel	* Col. ML2085
" 'Tis the Last Rose of Summer"	MENDELSSOHN	R. Kyriakou	Vox VBX412
" 'Twas Within a Furlong of Edinborough Town"	PURCELL	J. Shirley-Quirk	Saga (Eng.) XID5260; STXID5260

"Maggie Lauder"	HAYDN	D. Fischer-Dieskau	* DGG 18706; 138706
"Bonnie Laddie, Highland Lad- die"	BEETHOVEN	R. Dyer-Bennet	* Conc.H. CHC13
"Come Fill, Fill My Good Fel- low"	BEETHOVEN	D. Fischer-Dieskau	* DGG 18706; 138706
"True-Hearted Was He" (listed as "A Fortunate Lover")	WEBER	D. Fischer-Dieskau	* DGG 18706; 138706
"Where Ha'e Ye Been A' The Day" (listed as "Glowing Love")	WEBER	D. Fischer-Dieskau	*DGG 18706; 138706
"The Banjo"	GOTTSCHALK	E. List A. Rigai F. Glazer A. Mandel	Vanguard 485 Decca DL710143 Conc.D. 1217/217 Desto 6470/3
"A Son of a Gambolier"	IVES	Lehigh University Band	Lehigh 1134
"My Shepherd Will Supply My Need"	THOMSON	Mormon Tabernacle Choir	Col ML5767; MS6367
"The Dodger"	COPLAND	W. Warfield	Col ML5897; MS6497

KEY: Col.   = Columbia
       Conc. H. = Concert Hall Soc.
       Conc. D. = Concert Disc
       Cor.   = Coral
       DGG   = Deutsch Grammophon Gesellschaft
       DYB   = Dyer-Bennet
       Ois.   = Oiseau-Lyre

   * Out of Print
   ** 45 rpm